MINUTE GUIDE TO

SHORT-TERM RETIREMENT PLANNING

by Mark Battersby

Macmillan Spectrum/Alpha Books

A Division of Macmillan General Reference
A Simon & Schuster Macmillan Company
1633 Broadway, New York, NY 10019

International Standard Book Number: 0-02-861181-0
Library of Congress Catalog Card Number: A catalog record of this publication is available through the Library of Congress.

98 97 96   8 7 6 5 4 3 2 1

Interpretation of the printing code: the rightmost double-digit number is the year of the book's first printing; the rightmost single-digit number is the number of the book's printing. For example, a printing code of 96-1 shows that this copy of the book was printed during the first printing of the book in 1996.

Printed in the United States of America

Note: Reasonable care has been taken in the preparation of the text to ensure its clarity and accuracy. This book is sold with the understanding that the author and the publisher are not engaged in rendering legal, accounting, or other professional service. Laws vary from state to state, and readers with specific financial questions should seek the services of a professional adviser.

The author and publisher specifically disclaim any liability, loss of risk, personal or otherwise, which is incurred as a consequence, directly or indirectly, of the use and application of any of the contents of this book.

Publisher: Theresa Murtha
Development Editor: Debra Wishik Englander
Production Editor: Theresa Mathias
Cover Designer: Dan Armstrong
Designer: Barb Kordesh
Indexer: Chris Wilcox
Production Team: Angela Calvert, Kim Cofer, David Garratt,
                Erich J. Richter, Christy Wagner

CONTENTS

INTRODUCTION

As you begin planning for retirement, you face a tremendous number of decisions. You must consider the benefits offered by your employer, your personal finances, as well as many unexpected stumbling blocks. Those stumbling blocks may result from family emergencies, unexpected unemployment, and even income tax rules. These factors make planning for retirement especially difficult.

The *10 Minute Guide to Short-Term Retirement Planning* will teach you the basics of retirement planning and the investment strategies you can employ to reach your goals. The lessons in this book will guide you through the complexities of employee benefit programs, tax rules, and the many investment options available to you.

CONVENTIONS USED IN THIS BOOK

Each lesson will take about 10 minutes or so for you to complete. To help you progress through the lessons, the *10 Minute Guide to Short-Term Retirement Planning* uses the following elements to emphasize important information:

 Plain English. Defines new or unfamiliar terms in "plain English."

> **tip** These are ideas that will help you avoid confusion by showing you the methods used by others and alternative ways of reaching your goal of a successful retirement.

> **!** This element will highlight common problems you may face.

WHAT TO DO NOW

Start by reviewing the table of contents. Depending on the type of retirement planning you have already started, you may want to go to a particular lesson. Otherwise, start with Lesson 1, "Planning for Retirement." By reading the entire book, you will understand the tools, weapons, and strategies you need to retire. You will better understand how much help you can expect from your employer. Most importantly, you will discover the broad array of investment options available to help you achieve the retirement goals you have learned to establish.

PLANNING FOR RETIREMENT

In this lesson, you will learn the basics of planning for retirement and how to take full advantage of all your sources of retirement funds, especially if you're planning to retire in ten years or less.

RETIREMENT FACTS

According to a recent survey by the Employee Benefits Research Institute (EBRI), 28 percent of respondents age 55 or older had not yet begun to save for their retirement. Only 31 percent of workers age 55 or older who are currently working are receiving, have received, or expect to receive a private- or public-sector pension.

WHEN DO YOU PLAN TO RETIRE?

It's never too late to plan for a secure retirement. Today, you're faced with two significant developments that will have a major impact on your retirement planning process:

- This is the era of corporate downsizing.
- The baby-boomers are reaching the age of 50 in record numbers.

Regardless of your age, you may be forced into retirement before you're ready. And, unless you retire within the next few years, the baby-boomer generation that is now turning 50 may exhaust the public-sector retirement benefits.

HOW LONG WILL YOUR RETIREMENT LAST?

The average life expectancy in the 1940s was roughly age 69. Today, the average life span is about 78 years. However, even that figure can play a statistical trick on your retirement planning.

If you make it to age 65, chances are you're going to live past 78. Today, men who live to 65 will probably see age 80; women who achieve retirement age will likely live to about 85. Improvements in longevity suggest that the chances of a relatively long retirement are quite high. A longer retirement and a relatively short period of time in which to plan for it means that additional resources will be required to meet monthly expenditures, pay increased medical bills, and protect against inflation.

HOW MUCH WILL PENSIONS AND SOCIAL SECURITY PROVIDE?

As the baby-boomer generation ages, it's unlikely that Social Security will provide the same level of benefits that it has in the past. The ever-dwindling number of workers paying into the system combined with an ever-growing number of retirees will place an increasing burden on private-sector retirement plans.

While new employer retirement plans are allowing employees to take greater control of their retirement planning, these plans also require considerably more vigilance on the part of the employee.

How can you acquire those needed retirement resources without risking everything? The key is capital preservation.

HOW MUCH HAVE YOU CURRENTLY SET ASIDE FOR RETIREMENT?

After the age of 40, retirement savings can no longer be considered discretionary; it's no longer an incidental element in an otherwise solid retirement plan revolving around Social Security and an employer sponsored pension. Instead, increased retirement savings have become an almost indispensable component of a total retirement portfolio.

IS A RETIREMENT PLAN REALLY NECESSARY?

Many people neglect to plan for their retirement and end up either working beyond their desired retirement age or living a financially troubled retirement. Overlooking the importance of retirement planning after you have reached the age of 40 can make achieving the goal of retirement an impossible dream. Just think, you can expect to spend one-third of your life retired...you had better hope your retirement savings last that long.

tip To maintain the same standard of living in retirement that you enjoy today, you will need an annual retirement income of approximately 75 percent of the amount you currently spend.

WHAT WILL RETIREMENT COST?

To come to grips with the cost of retirement, one of the most important questions you must consider is what type of retirement you want. In other words, when planning for retirement you must first understand what your goal is; how much will you need to spend in order to support yourself during retirement?

You might answer this question with a simple "who knows"— especially if you have many years to go before you retire. However, the cost of retirement is generally based on three questions:

- When will you retire?
- How much will you need?
- How long will you need it?

tip On the plus side, remember that the bigger the retirement spending goal is, the greater the rate of inflation, and the more years to retirement, the worse it gets, at least for those with many years to go until retirement. Those with fewer years to go until retirement, of course, will be affected less by these outside factors.

TODAY'S DOLLARS VERSUS FUTURE DOLLARS

With relatively few years to go until retirement, at least compared to someone just starting out, "future dollars" will not be all that much different from "today's dollars." Those future dollars, the value of a dollar years down the road, do deserve attention.

In the coming lessons, you will see amounts in today's dollars (today's purchasing power) wherever possible instead of future dollars (what things will cost tomorrow).

If you are wondering where your future income will come from, consider this table from a study done on today's retired and the sources of their retirement income:

Retirement Income Sources

Social Security	44%
Pensions and investments	43%
Employment	10%
Other	3%

Source: Employee Benefits Research Institute

PLANNING TO MEET FUTURE EXPENSES

Your retirement planning should have a specific goal in financial terms and in terms of a desired lifestyle. For example, you plan to be mortgage-free by the time you're ready to retire. If you can be mortgage-free or have a very low mortgage by the time you retire, your living expenses will be considerably lower than if you remain tied to a large mortgage or rent payment.

! Don't include the value of your home in the retirement-related assets section of your retirement plan unless you plan to sell the house and downsize or become a renter when you retire.

In addition, don't include the value of your personal property (automobiles, furniture, and so on). Even if you have a collectible car, chances are that it won't be worth what you expect if you decide to sell it.

The whole idea of retirement planning is to go from where you are now to where you want or need to be at the time you want to retire (or are forced to retire). The fact that the number of years between now and that point in time is steadily declining is no reason to panic.

ANALYZE YOUR RETIREMENT PLAN

The key here is to decide on reasonable goals for your retirement. During the process, ask yourself broad, general questions. From the answers to those questions, you will form realistic goals that can be achieved using the strategies and tools you'll read about in later lessons. As additional information becomes available to you during the period between now and retirement, you will continue to narrow your investment options and maneuver to take full advantage of all the resources available to help you in retirement.

The advantage to this approach is that you end up with manageable problems to solve instead of an overwhelming feeling that leads to a "whatever happens, happens" approach. Or, even worse, feeling that those retirement goals are out of reach at this late date.

In this lesson, you learned how important it is to plan early. You learned how to consider all the variables involved in retirement planning. You also learned about the potential problems an unexpected, forced retirement or an early retirement could cause. In the next lesson, you will learn about the potential pitfalls as well as some of the tools you need to reach your goal of a financially secure and worry-free retirement.

THE STARTING LINE

In this lesson, you will learn how to evaluate your financial status by looking through your financial records and by taking a personal inventory of your assets.

WHERE ARE YOU TODAY?

To assess what you have, you need to take a look at the following three areas:

- **Your Own Financial Resources.** These include assets such as your house, cars, personal property, money you have in the bank, and the value of your investments. This also includes protections you have in the form of life insurance or disability insurance policies.

- **Employer-Paid Benefits.** You may already be entitled to a monthly pension benefit when you retire.

- **Social Security Benefits.** You can expect a retirement benefit from Social Security that will replace a portion of your pre-retirement earnings. Social

Security also provides disability benefits if you're totally disabled and survivor benefits if you die with children at home up to high school age.

ASSESSING YOUR RESOURCES

Preparing a personal financial summary will help you understand where you stand financially. This summary should have two parts: a balance sheet and a cash flow statement.

 Balance Sheet. The balance sheet is a snapshot of your financial condition as of a single date, such as the last day of the year. It lists what you have and what you owe.

You can also think of a balance sheet as a list of the following:

- The value of your assets, such as investments, your home, and your car.
- The amount of your liabilities, such as mortgage loans and credit card balances.
- Your net worth, which is simply the difference between your assets and your liabilities.

 Cash Flow Statement. A cash flow statement measures your cash infusions (income) and your cash outflows (expenses) over a period of time, usually a year. The difference between your income and your expenses represents the amount available for investment and savings.

SOURCES OF RETIREMENT INCOME

The following are traditional sources of retirement income:

- Social Security
- Company retirement plans
- Company-sponsored savings plans, such as Simplified Employee Pension (SEP) plans and 401(k) plans
- Personal savings
- Individual Retirement Accounts (IRAs)
- Annuities
- Investments
- Part-time work during retirement
- Proceeds from the sale of a home
- Cash value life insurance

> **!** Social Security benefits will replace a relatively small portion of the income of upper-income retirees in the years ahead. That is, if your earnings have consistently been in the top Social Security bracket, you can expect benefits to equal only about 24 percent ($14,388) of the portion of your pay that is subject to Social Security tax ($61,200 in 1995).

> **!** As much as 85 percent of the Social Security benefits to higher-income retirees may be subject (under current laws) to federal income tax.

IS IT TOO LATE TO QUALIFY FOR SOCIAL SECURITY?

Your earnings determine the amount of Social Security benefits you will ultimately receive. The more you earn, the more you will receive, although there are certain maximum contribution and benefit limits. The law bases your retirement benefits on your average earnings for a 35-year period, but don't worry if you don't have 35 more years to work.

You're eligible for benefits if you're what the Social Security Administration calls "fully insured," meaning that you have built up 40 calendar quarters of coverage. In 1995, you receive a calendar quarter of coverage for every $630 per quarter you earn up to a maximum of four quarters each year.

When you have worked the 40 quarters (the equivalent of 10 years), you are fully insured for life—and entitled to benefits even if you never work again.

SAFEGUARDING YOUR RETIREMENT

You should already be investing for retirement. If, like most of us, you haven't yet begun saving for the future, it's important to quickly build up those retirement savings. Building a retirement nest egg, however, should not be done in a panic. It's vital that you protect the surprising number of assets you're just now beginning to discover you have—and don't forget to consider all of the factors that will affect your retirement income.

HELP FROM YOUR EMPLOYER

After the age of 40, you should also be taking full advantage of employer-provided benefit plans, not only to supplement your Social Security benefits but to help make up the shortfall that will almost certainly occur when you discover that Social Security won't provide all of the income you require in retirement. You'll read more about the options offered by employers and see how to make the best use of those employer-provided benefits in reaching your retirement goals in later lessons.

INFLATION

Inflation could best be compared to a tax on savings and investments. The bite that inflation takes out of savings and the return from those savings must be considered in even short-term retirement planning.

Rising prices (and, hopefully, your still rising income) will impact your future spending needs and your future financial resources. Failing to consider inflation may leave you wide of the mark in reaching your financial goals. Of course, thinking in terms of inflated dollars a number of years down the road can lead to quite a shock.

Fortunately, a dollar received today is worth more than a dollar received in the future. Why?

Today's dollar can be invested and thus earn a return. The levels of real returns that are available from different types of investments vary over time depending on the relationship between inflation and nominal investment returns.

Stocks in recent years have usually generated substantial real returns (the rate of return minus the rate of inflation). In contrast, real returns for money market funds and bank certificates of deposit (CDs) are generally lower.

COMPOUNDING

The mechanics of compound interest enables you to project the impact of time on money, such as the money you expect to save and spend in the years ahead. For example, you can use the mathematics of compound interest to estimate your living costs over the period of years when you expect to be retired.

Likewise, you can use it to figure how much to save each year in order to build a certain nest egg by retirement and to estimate how many years it will last.

Compound Interest. Compound interest is interest earned on principal plus interest earned earlier.

Future Value. The amount to which an investment will grow at some point in the future if it earns a specified interest rate that is compounded annually. The process of calculating future value is called compounding.

THE RULE OF 72

You can explore the interplay of time and return with the "Rule of 72." When money doubles over a certain period of time, the product of the number of compounding periods and the rate of return per period will equal approximately 72. Therefore, if you pick an annual rate of return and divide it into 72, the answer will be a close approximation of the number of years required for your money to double.

In this lesson, you learned about the importance of a cash flow statement and a balance sheet as well as what you have to consider when preparing your own financial statements. You also learned about the various sources of retirement income available. In the next lesson, you will learn how to set retirement goals.

YOUR RETIREMENT GOALS

In this lesson, you will learn the importance of establishing goals for your retirement plan.

TIME HORIZONS

Retirement planning involves two important factors: your financial position today and your financial position after retirement. After all, there is a unique time horizon—the period over which you will accumulate money for those goals and the period over which those accumulated funds will be spent. The goal, obviously, is a financially secure retirement at a comfortable standard of living.

BEGINNING GOAL SETTING

You can begin developing your retirement goals simply by making a list, then reviewing and refining it as you go. First, describe your goals in qualitative terms only, then begin to revise them. You might, for example, consider the following list of basic questions. Your answers will form the basis for establishing your retirement goals.

- How much money will you really need to maintain the lifestyle you want and where will it come from?

- What can you do now to make sure you will have enough money to provide a financially secure retirement?

- What will Social Security provide?

- Do you really want to quit work altogether? Can you afford to?

- What investment, tax savings, credit, and insurance strategies will help you put together the best worry-free retirement plan?

- How can you keep medical costs from wiping you out financially?

EVER-CHANGING GOALS

Periodically revising your retirement goals will make each goal increasingly specific and measurable. You should be able to revise each goal two or three times without stating it in terms of a particular dollar amount. Instead, express your goals as a percentage of your current income or current living expenses.

Thinking of your goals in terms of today's dollars makes it easy to compare them to your present level of income and investments.

IGNORING THE UNTHINKABLE

When looking at your long-term spending needs, you may be tempted to assume that if you live to your 80s or beyond someone else will help pay for your needs. However, that's no longer a sensible approach. It's essential that you start preparing now.

Planning for retirement represents the biggest challenge because your retirement time horizon extends decades into the
future—and the future is full of uncertainties. You don't know
the length of that time horizon and you don't know your life
expectancy. The extended life horizon makes forecasting less
reliable. As a result, your retirement goals and the strategies
you develop to reach those goals are a "first shot" that will
have to be revised many times as the future unfolds.

tip   For every dollar you don't save for retirement by
the age of 35, you will need to put aside almost
four dollars at age 55 (assuming a seven percent
rate of return in your investments).

tip   Keep in mind that the lower your current income,
the more likely you are to need a greater percentage of it during retirement. For people who currently have household income under $50,000,
many financial planners assume a retirement goal
as high as 90 percent of current income.

WHEN SHOULD YOU RETIRE?

The easy answer to this question is when you're ready. In
today's business climate, however, it isn't that simple. By planning for an early retirement, say at age 55 instead of 65, you
are in a sense ensuring that you can meet your retirement
goals even if your job is eliminated.

HOW MUCH WILL YOU SPEND DURING RETIREMENT?

Although you may estimate what you will spend during retirement as a percentage of your current income, that figure can be refined quite easily. If you're close to retirement age, determining the goal is fairly easy because you know what you're spending your money on today.

INFLATION

Even though most economists feel that inflation will remain relatively low over the next 20 years (averaging four to six percent annually), don't think that a low rate won't affect you.

Rising prices (and rising incomes) will affect both your future spending needs and future resources. Failure to take inflation into account can leave you behind in reaching your retirement goals.

TODAY'S LIFESTYLE

One way to set retirement goals is to use your lifestyle today as a guideline. No one can predict the future, but you know how you live today and what things cost today. Simply plan for a long-range goal that approximates today's lifestyle.

> *tip*   One easy rule of thumb is to plan for an average spending goal of 60 to 80 percent of your current spending and income during retirement and then refine it as you go along.

How Will Your Spending Change During Retirement?

Experts explain retirement as having three broad phases: active, less active, and passive. In the early years of your retirement, you are apt to be very active, spending a great deal on travel and entertainment. As the years go by, you're likely to become less active and you will see your activities and lifestyle change. Then, depending on your broad family plans and whether you have long-term care insurance, your passive years will probably see your spending increase again as medical and long-term care expenses increase.

Change Today for Tomorrow's Lifestyle?

How much should you adapt or change your current spending to reflect your post-retirement needs when establishing retirement goals? Not too surprisingly, it varies. For example, you probably won't be commuting, so car expenses will decline.

You will probably spend less on clothes. Personal loans or a home mortgage may be paid off by retirement—and you may want to plan to save during retirement. If you don't work during retirement, you won't pay any Social Security taxes. Because of lower income, income taxes should decrease.

In this lesson, you learned the importance of setting goals and revising them as circumstances dictate. In the next lesson, you will learn more about your basic assets.

Asset Evaluation

In this lesson, you will learn how to evaluate the assets you now have.

Evaluating What You Have

At this stage in the retirement planning process take a look at some of the more familiar assets described here to get an idea of the role they will play in the retirement planning process.

Your Home

The equity in your home is not usually considered available until you reach the age of 55. That's the earliest you can take up to $125,000 of profit tax-free.

You can, of course, sell your home at any time and use the equity for your early retirement; however, doing so before age 55 results in a capital gains tax (a substantial tax penalty) and, in turn, a loss of funds to your retirement nest egg.

SELLING DOWN

You may want to exploit the financial value of the equity in your home and invest it to speed up your retirement planning. Because of a one-time, $125,000 capital gains tax exclusion available to those 55 or older, you may be able to trade down to a smaller home and free up a substantial amount of money from the proceeds of the sale to add to your retirement investment portfolio.

This strategy is particularly attractive if you are age 55 and older because you can take advantage of the one-time tax exclusion on capital gains of up to $125,000 from the sale of a home. To be eligible, neither you nor your spouse can have used the exclusion before and the home must have been your principal residence for at least three of the five years before the sale date.

To defer any gain over the $125,000 one time tax exclusion, the price of the new residence must be equal to or greater than the price of your old residence and you must buy and occupy that new residence within 24 months before or after selling your old home.

REVERSE MORTGAGES

Reverse mortgage loans are a new form of mortgage that allows you to convert the equity in your home into installment payments that could provide you with monthly income for life.

 Reverse Mortgage. A reverse mortgage is when you borrow against your property. Instead of receiving the proceeds in a lump sum, they are paid to you in installments.

As an alternative, you often have the option of getting the proceeds from a reverse mortgage either in the form of regular payments for a predetermined period of time or in the form of a credit line against which you can withdraw money when you want or need it. When you die or move from your house, your reverse equity loan immediately becomes due.

Because there are no monthly payments due for a reverse mortgage, you don't need a salary or other earnings to qualify. The amount of monthly income you can obtain from a reverse mortgage depends on several factors, including your age, the prevailing interest rates, and the value of your property.

Usually, reverse mortgages are only available for borrowers age 62 or older. Naturally, the older you are when you apply for your reverse mortgage, the higher the monthly payments you will receive.

ASSET ALLOCATION

A decision you have to make involves deciding how to best use the assets you already possess. How you apportion your money among cash, bonds, stocks, and hard assets will determine your investment return.

Asset Allocation. This is the proper mix of investments in your investment portfolio.

Focusing on asset allocation can help you reach your retirement goal in the relatively short period of time you have before retirement. Stock and bonds prices, for example, will usually fluctuate over time. Instead of focusing on the ups and downs, however, concentrate on maintaining the proper mix among the asset categories in your retirement nest egg.

SAVINGS VERSUS INVESTING

You may not think there's a difference between saving for retirement and investing for retirement. After all, both words cover the process of putting away money for retirement. However, saving money means not spending it; investing money, on the other hand, means taking money you have saved and earning a return on it.

RISK

With little time before retirement, you may find yourself pressed to seek higher returns from your investments in order to attain your retirement goals. This usually means increased risk.

 Risk. Risk is the possibility of losing money. If the price of an asset can go down, then the investment involves some degree of risk.

 Return. Return is the gain you make on an investment. It's your earnings and how much you are ahead.

FULLY INSURED SAVINGS RISK-FREE?

Bank accounts up to the $100,000 Federal Deposit Insurance Corporation's (FDIC) insurance limit are free of one type of risk: the risk of loss of principal and interest. However, those insured savings are vulnerable to purchasing power risk, which is the chance that money invested in them will have less purchasing power in the future than it does today.

tip For every dollar you don't save for retirement by age 40, you will need to put aside $4.00 at age 55, assuming a seven percent rate of return on your investments.

SELF-DEFEATING RISK

Treasury bills and federally insured bank accounts are good examples of hidden risks you may not be aware of. Your principal and interest are both guaranteed by the government (up to insurance limits), but your return may not keep pace with inflation.

In this lesson, you learned the importance of evaluating your assets to make the best use of them in reaching your retirement goals. In the next lesson, you will learn how to chart a course to your retirement goals.

GETTING THERE WITHOUT PANIC

In this lesson, you will learn that it isn't what you earn that will guarantee a comfortable retirement, it's what you're able to save and earn from those investments.

ADDING TO YOUR RETIREMENT FUNDS

You can acquire the savings you need for your retirement by simply diverting a portion of your income between now and retirement. Those savings can come from the return on your retirement savings and investments or by reducing your current expenses.

WHERE DOES THE MONEY GO?

Before you can increase your savings or find more money for savings, you must attempt to pinpoint where your money goes now. As you have seen, that means keeping records. Documenting rent or mortgage payments, utilities, car payments, furniture, and other major purchases is a big part of your record keeping. Also consider the following questions:

- How do you spend your pocket money?
- How do you spend those $100 withdrawals from the ATM?

* What were those department store and credit charges for?

If you don't know the answers to these questions, you aren't keeping track of your day-to-day spending. Cash flow statements and even a budget will help in this area.

> *tip* Think of saving for retirement as just one more monthly expense. Shoot for 15 percent of your net income. That 15 percent figure shouldn't put too much strain on your finances and should provide a reasonable starting point for retirement savings.

REFINANCE WHEN MORTGAGE RATES ARE LOW

If the interest rate on your mortgage is relatively high, re-financing may lop off $100, $300, or more from your monthly payment. However, when you switch to a cheaper mortgage, don't let the savings slip away. Each time you write a check for your mortgage payment, write a second check for the amount of money saved and add it to your retirement nest egg.

TAP TAX BREAKS FOR SELF-EMPLOYED

If you're self-employed, consider arranging your business to take advantage of home-office tax deductions. Put the money you save into your retirement plan.

If you aren't self-employed, consider starting a for-profit, side-line business that will allow you to capture the same home-office tax deductions while creating extra income.

As an added bonus, you can open a Keogh retirement plan and make tax-deductible contributions of up to 20 percent of your self-employment income.

GOOD DEBT VERSUS BAD DEBT

Not all debt is bad. The idea is to eliminate all unnecessary debt. Necessary debt can include a mortgage, car loans, and money borrowed to pay for education. These debts, managed properly, can be strategic financial moves aimed at helping you reach your retirement planning goals.

The other type of debt is the unnecessary, discretionary variety that often tends to show up as creeping credit card balances, installment loans, and other revolving-credit type debt.

Depending on your financial circumstances, eliminating all debt may not be possible or even desirable. Borrowing does have strategic advantages at times: you can use it as an asset to boost your wealth through leverage, to handle a financial emergency, or to speed up a necessary purchase.

KEEPING DEBT TO A MINIMUM

How do you keep debts down?

- **Try to pay off your mortgage early.** Don't worry about fancy formulas. Simply pay a little extra principal each month on your mortgage payment. Any amount—$25, $50, $100—will do. Each time you make a mortgage prepayment, you are investing the money at the same rate the mortgage company has been charging you.

The savings generated by prepaying are dramatic. If you and your spouse are 40 years old, and you just purchased a home with a 30-year, $100,000 mortgage at 10 percent interest, your monthly payment is about $870, not counting any payments for taxes or insurance. By adding only $31 to the monthly mortgage payment, you can reduce the term of the mortgage by almost five years. The extra $9,300 you invest through those $31 monthly additions will knock $43,300 off of what you would have to pay in interest over the life of the loan.

• **Save a bundle on credit card interest.** Among all types of consumer debt, credit card debt is the most expensive and the most damaging to any retirement plan. The real cost of rising balances on credit cards is an eye-opener. If you make the minimum two percent payment on a credit card that charges a $20 annual fee and 19.8 percent interest, it will take you 31 years and a total of $7,700 to pay off a $2,000 balance.

• **Tap the tax benefits of home equity credit.** When borrowing is necessary, your plan should be to find the cheapest possible source of credit. For anyone who owns a home with enough built-in equity, the least expensive credit source is almost always a home equity loan or line of credit.

Home Equity Loan. A home equity loan or line of credit is when you borrow against the value of your home.

Whether fixed-term loans or revolving lines of credit, home equity loans are today's debt of choice because interest rates are among the lowest available and the interest you pay is usually fully tax-deductible for loans up to $100,000.

- **Stop taking out car loans.** A car loan is probably your second largest debt outside a home mortgage. With auto loans being stretched to four or five years, by the time you pay it off, you may well need another loan to buy another car.

One way to break free is to use home equity credit to pay for your next car. Assuming a prime rate of 7 percent, for example, you could buy your vehicle with an 8.5-percent home equity loan, which makes your after-tax cost just 6.12 percent (assuming that you're in the 28 percent tax bracket).

Chances are that you will still be driving your vehicle after the loan is paid. But don't stop making monthly payments. Steer that $300 to $400 into your nest egg account each month until it is time to buy another car.

TAX-DEFERRED SAVINGS

The benefits of tax-deferred savings far outweigh the lost flexibility and potential penalties. This is because you can build up your retirement assets in tax-deferred accounts much more quickly than you can with a savings account that is not tax-favored. The best of all worlds is to save with pretax dollars (or get a current tax deduction for the money you put into the tax deferred arrangement).

HOW MUCH FASTER CAN YOU ACCUMULATE MONEY?

For those over age 40 and planning retirement, speed is of the essence. Let's say that each year for the next 25 years you plan to contribute $8,000 of your earnings to a taxable investment with an average annual return of 8 percent. But you actually only put $5,520 away because you first have to pay income taxes on your earnings. Those taxes add up to $2,480 a year (31 percent times $8,000). At the end of 25 years (after you pay your taxes each year), your investment will have grown to $269,793.

What if you set aside the same amount each year in a tax-favored, employer-sponsored 401(k) plan and your dollars earned the same return (8 percent) annually for 25 years? With your money in that 401(k), your earnings build up tax-deferred. You have the full $8,000 to put away because you can put the money into the plan before taxes. In 25 years, you would have an impressive $584,847 (or $315,054 more).

Let's say you withdraw your money in a single sum and pay taxes at 31 percent. You would still have $373,574, or $101,955 more than you would have had outside a tax-deferred savings plan.

With retirement so close, it's a good idea to put the money from any tax-deferred accounts into a rollover IRA at retirement. You can take money out as you need it and, therefore, pay taxes only on the money you withdraw at the time you withdraw it.

In this lesson, you learned that some debt may be necessary to achieve quick growth in your retirement nest egg. In the next lesson, you will learn how to protect the assets you now have and those you will soon acquire.

PROTECTION

In this lesson, you will learn the importance of protecting your current assets and those you will acquire between now and retirement.

YOU DON'T HAVE THE LUXURY OF TIME

After the age of 40, protecting what you have is extremely important because you don't have extra years to make up for devastating setbacks, such as those caused by unforeseen emergencies, loss of money from illness, or loss of value of investments if the stock market takes a drop. As retirement approaches or if a relatively short period of time exists before retirement, then riskier, higher-yielding investments may be necessary in order to achieve those goals.

LIFE INSURANCE

The most important asset in your retirement plan obviously is you. If your demise would result in economic hardship for your spouse or other loved ones, you're a candidate for life insurance.

Life Insurance. Life insurance is insurance that provides income to your survivors in the event of your death.

tip If the payoff from life insurance is invested at a reasonable rate, your family should have enough to carry on without you, after accounting for amounts available from Social Security and other assets you manage to accumulate.

INSURANCE CHOICES

Although there are many life insurance companies, there are really only two types of policies:

- **Term Life Insurance.** This insurance is pure and simple; it doesn't have any complicated investment or tax-deferred savings features attached.

- **Cash Value or Whole Life Insurance.** These are policies where your life coverage doubles as a retirement savings vehicle that offers the advantage of tax-deferred money growth over the long term.

If you already have trouble finding enough money to fund your 401(k) or IRA to the maximum each year, you should not shell out big money for cash value insurance coverage. Cash value insurance coverage is laden with high up-front costs, an uncertain investment return, and a large "early surrender" penalty if you try to cash in the policy before 10 years or so.

Naturally, if you have an existing cash value policy that already has a built-up cash value, you would probably be wise to hang on to it. By now, that policy may be providing coverage at a very reasonable cost compared with what you would pay for a newly issued term policy.

TERM LIFE INSURANCE

Term life insurance is the simplest and cheapest form of life insurance; it offers the most coverage for the lowest cost. You select the level of coverage you want—$50,000, $500,000, or any other amount—and pay an annual premium. If you die while you own the policy, your beneficiaries receive the money.

The premium is based on the amount of insurance coverage, your general health, and your age when you first buy the policy. The premium rises as you grow older. A 40-year-old nonsmoker in good health, for example, can buy a $250,000, one-year policy for about $360 per year to start. A 50-year-old nonsmoker buying the same policy would start at about $808 per year.

With some policies, the premium rises each year; with others, the premium is fixed for five-year periods. The 40-year-old's premium under a policy similar to the one mentioned, for example, would be $400 for five years, $600 for the next five years, $920 for the next five years, and so on. Most plans are guaranteed renewable as long as you keep paying the premiums. To keep on track, be sure the policy you choose includes that renewal feature.

CASH VALUE INSURANCE

For most retirement plans, term life is terrific. But cash value insurance coverage can be a sound addition if the following conditions are true:

- You need lots of insurance, such as more than $750,000.

- You're already contributing the maximum to IRAs for you and your spouse, to a 401(k) plan if you qualify, or any other tax-sheltered retirement savings plan available to you.

- You can afford it—which is to say that you're probably earning more than $150,000 per year.

A portion of what you pay in premiums each year goes to pay for the life insurance coverage, but the bulk of the money is devoted to the savings and investment features that are intended to build cash value for your nest egg.

Remember, though, this type of policy has a value that increases over time and that you can tap for retirement income. It's very similar to a tax-favored savings plan with life insurance attached. Part of your premium pays for insurance, part goes to your savings, and investment earnings are allowed to accumulate tax-free.

> **!** Because commissions and fees take such a large bite out of your cash value during the first few years, you need to keep funding a policy for at least 10 years for your investment to pay off.

MEDICAL INSURANCE

Some type of medical insurance is a must to avoid having to divert savings and earnings away from building up your retirement nest egg because of medical expenses.

If you have employer-sponsored medical health coverage—either through your company or your spouse's—making the most of it now, before retirement, can free up resources for your retirement plan. Investigate the coverage you and your spouse have now. You may be able to save thousands of dollars each year by better insurance benefits management.

> **!** Before you cancel any insurance, however, find out the conditions under which you will be allowed to rejoin the group if your other coverage is ever in jeopardy.

DISABILITY INSURANCE

Although you probably don't want to think about needing disability coverage, statistics show that you're far more likely to suffer a disability than you think.

If you have assets or future income to protect, disability insurance is coverage you can't afford to overlook. First, review you employer's coverage to see what the policy covers. If your employer's policy is not sufficient, then you need to look into getting your own policy.

Long-term disability insurance protects you and your family against the loss of income due to prolonged illness or crippling injury. Generally, the shorter the term of disability, the less the expense. However, the longer the term of the disability, the greater the need for adequate coverage.

Depending on how much income your asset base can generate, your disability coverage should provide benefits that equal 60 to 80 percent of your current gross income. Your coverage should guarantee benefits until you either recover or reach age 65 (when you will be eligible for Social Security benefits).

There are two types of disability insurance: any occupation coverage and own occupation coverage. The first kind will take effect only should your disability prevent you from working at even the simplest, most menial, low-paying job. The second kind takes effect if your disability prevents you from working at your own occupation. For obvious reasons, you should make sure that your disability insurance provides own occupation coverage.

You also need to know about the elimination period. This is the time that elapses between the onset of the disability and the beginning of the benefit period. During the elimination period, you must be able to pay for your own expenses. As long as you can afford to cover a period of disability out of your own pocket, you can opt for a longer elimination period.

Private disability insurance is designed to pay you a monthly benefit if you become disabled.

MEDICARE AND MEDIGAP INSURANCE IN YOUR FUTURE

Once you reach the age of 65, Uncle Sam will step into the health insurance picture with Medicare, which will pay a portion of your health costs in retirement—but only a portion. You will also need Medigap coverage, which is paid for either by your former employer or by you, to cover what Medicare doesn't.

Once fraught with confusion and fraud, Medigap insurance was radically revamped and a crop of new, simpler policies was introduced in 1992. Current annual premiums range from about $450 per year for a basic Medigap policy to $1,750 for Cadillac coverage.

LONG-TERM CARE INSURANCE

One of the major limitations of the Medicare program is that it excludes coverage for basic (or custodial) nursing home care, which now averages about $30,000 a year. To prepare for this potential liability, you can now buy long-term care insurance.

 Long-Term Care Insurance. Long-term care insurance policies provide for your daily expenses, ranging from $30 to $250, to cover nursing home or nursing care costs.

While premium rates vary depending on the level of benefits desired, such coverage will usually be more expensive if you wait until after retirement to sign up.

In this lesson, you learned how to take advantage of long-term savings opportunities and to continue to develop strategies for protecting the financial health of your family. In the next lesson, you will learn which professional advisers you may want to consult as you plan for your retirement.

GETTING THE INFORMATION YOU NEED

In this lesson, you will learn about using available information and professional assistance to help plan your retirement.

USING PROFESSIONAL ADVISERS

Finding a competent adviser is well worth the effort. There is no ideal way to locate those professionals, but word of mouth recommendations can be an important first step. Some types of investments, such as stocks and bonds, can only be purchased through licensed brokers; CDs and savings accounts require the services and advice of a banker; and insurance-related investments require insurance agents or brokers.

TAKING ADVANTAGE OF PROFESSIONAL MONEY MANAGERS

Some advisers and professionals come with the investment, such as a professional money manager. For example, you may come in contact with a professional money manager through a mutual fund. Don't overlook managers who work with individual portfolios.

Money Manager. A money manager is someone who receives a fee to manage your money. The money manager can be self-employed, or he or she can work for a mutual fund, bank, or investment company.

A professional money manager can custom-design an individual portfolio for you that reflects your specific investment goals and objectives. The services of professional money managers were once available only to very wealthy individual investors. Today, growing numbers of people can take advantage of their services.

Money management services are available from independent managers, trust or private banking departments, financial planners, and stockbrokers. A professional money manager is paid an annual fee, which is typically a percentage of the assets under management.

! Fees for money managers can run from .75 percent to as high as 3 percent of the amount of money under management. Comparatively, the average for stock mutual funds is a 1.5 percent management fee.

! If you place assets with a money manager, you must trust the manager's judgment. Most accounts are handled on a fully discretionary basis, meaning the manager selects what to buy, when to buy it, and how much to buy.

WHAT ARE WRAP ACCOUNTS?

Since the mid-1980s, the brokerage industry has developed a service called the "wrap account," which allows you to receive professional money management services with as little as $100,000 in investible assets.

Wrap Account. A wrap account is simply a way to match you with a professional money manager who will handle the actual investment of your money. Thus, the broker from whom you buy the wrap account is seldom the person who will actually manage your money.

The term *wrap account* derives from the "wrap fee," an all-inclusive fee for money management, commissions/transaction charges, ongoing account monitoring, and service charges.

Wrap accounts are heavily promoted by brokerage firms, particularly for large lump-sum distributions that will be rolled over into IRAs. Most wrap fees start at 3 percent (with the average being 2.3 percent) of the money under management. These fees are often negotiable.

Wrap accounts seem like a great idea but may not be right for you. The wrap fee is often significantly higher than you might pay to other money management services on your own.

Overall, your decision to use a wrap account comes down to whether it is worth it to you to pay higher fees for personalized attention and professional money management. Those services might otherwise not be available based on your account balance. You will also have to weigh the value of your time and the effort of managing your own retirement portfolio or of using much lower-cost mutual funds against the higher fees of most wrap accounts.

In April of 1994, the Securities and Exchange Commission passed new rules governing the level of disclosure required of brokerage firms selling wrap accounts. Each firm is now required to disclose the following:

- Fee schedules, including what portion goes to the money manager and whether the fee is negotiable.

- How money managers are selected and reviewed, and the criteria used to judge performance.

- How performance numbers are calculated.

- Under what circumstances you will be allowed to contact the manager, such as if you must call the broker first.

- The amount of information the broker must give to the money manager about your investment goals and objectives, your risk tolerance, and so on.

USING FINANCIAL PLANNERS

A financial planner can be a valuable ally in reaching your retirement goals. You can link up with a planner on a continuing basis or pay for advice periodically as a kind of second opinion on your program.

A good financial planning professional can see to it that your investments are diversified and consistent with your retirement goals. A good planner can also help you anticipate the tax consequences of any financial decision that might affect your retirement nest egg.

Many planners are registered with the Securities and Exchange Commission (SEC) as investment advisers. This means that they can serve as money managers for their clients. They can create and manage investment portfolios, and charge a fee comparable to that charged by mutual funds.

Registered Investment Advisers. These individuals are registered with the Securities and Exchange Commission, which is required by law for people who give investment advice.

The fact that a planner is a certified member of a financial planning organization is a good starting point in finding a financial planner. There are three certificates that financial planners can have:

- **Accredited Personal Financial Specialist (APFS).** This certification is conferred by the American Institute of Certified Public Accountants (AICPA) and can be held only by CPAs. The majority of those with the APFS designation operate on a "fee only" basis, meaning that they charge a flat fee rather than depending on the commissions generated when they buy and sell investments for your account.

- **Certified Financial Planner (CFP).** The CFP designation is granted to individuals who have completed an intense study program, have passed a comprehensive examination, and have fulfilled an experience requirement.

- **Chartered Financial Consultant (ChFC).** This certification is awarded by the Bryn Mawr, Pennsylvania-based American Society of Chartered Life Underwriters (CLU) and Chartered Financial Consultants (ChFC) to individuals who complete a 10-section course of study and who have passed two examinations.

Financial planners are compensated for their efforts on your behalf through fees, commissions, or a combination of the two. A fee-only planner is paid on an hourly or a retainer basis. If a fee-only planner spends 10 hours devising an investment strategy for you, you are billed for 10 hours work at an hourly rate. Alternatively, the planner may arrange a fixed fee.

A commissioned planner earns his or her income by commissions charged as part of the cost of investments and insurance products you buy through the planner.

Some planners combine these two sources of compensation, earning income through both fees and commissions. Fees are earned by providing a review of your financial situation together with specific recommendations. If you decide to accept those recommendations, the planner will earn commissions on the investment and insurance products you purchase while implementing their recommendations.

DON'T FORGET THE CPAS

Certified Public Accountants, or CPAs, practice in every town in the country. A CPA provides a variety of services, and most are well-qualified to advise you on tax matters and to prepare your income taxes.

Many CPAs have also become proficient (and, as mentioned, even certified) in personal financial planning. The APFS degree designates a CPA who is qualified to help you with your personal financial planning needs.

OTHER PROFESSIONALS

Other professionals, such as bankers, insurance agents, or brokers and stockbrokers, who practice in specialty areas of retirement planning may also be able to assist you in attaining specific goals. An attorney is essential for preparing necessary estate planning documents such as your power of attorney and will.

> *tip*   It is often best to use an attorney who is approximately your age or younger because you don't want to have to find a new attorney when your current one retires.

You may, of course, outgrow your attorney's expertise if your investments and assets grow to a level that will require more sophisticated planning techniques.

In this lesson, you learned about using professional assistance to help formulate your retirement plan. In the next lesson, you will learn about the impact of income tax rules on your retirement planning.

USING TAX RULES AS A TOOL

In this lesson, you will learn how to take advantage of tax rules to bolster your retirement savings.

TAX STRATEGIES

Finding sensible ways to save on taxes is a good way to cut expenses—and increase retirement savings. Surprisingly, despite tax laws that defend the right of every individual to pay only minimum permissible taxes, many people pay more taxes than they have to.

MAKING TAX DEFERRAL WORK FOR YOU

Taxes work as a drag on the power of compounding by substantially reducing your effective rate of return. Because of taxes, you require significantly greater investment returns to reach your retirement goals.

If you are in the 31 percent tax bracket, for example, you will need a pretax return of 10.1 percent to attain an after-tax return of 7 percent. In the 36 percent bracket, you need a 10.9 percent pretax return to be able to keep 7 percent after taxes.

The best outcome where taxes are concerned, obviously, is not to have to pay them. That's a major reason why so many investors favor municipal bonds. Interest on municipal bonds is not generally subject to federal income taxes (although state or local income taxes may be due if you own municipal bonds issued outside your home state).

The Importance of Delaying Taxes—Legally

Investments not protected in tax-deferred assets are fully exposed to the eroding effects that rising tax rates have on long-term compounding. As a result, it usually makes sense to direct as much of your savings as possible into retirement accounts that offer shelter for pretax contributions, such as 401(k) plans.

Other savings vehicles, such as annuities, where you can obtain tax deferral on earnings but no up-front tax deduction on your contributions, may also make sense for you depending on your circumstances. Keep in mind, however, that higher costs and certain restrictions typically associated with annuities may offset some of the benefits of tax deferral.

Tax-Exempt Investments

You learn more about tax-free investments and the strategies for profiting from them in Lesson 14, for now you should be aware that you can benefit from investing in municipal securities.

Consider investing in tax-free securities if your taxable income is expected to place you in the 28 percent federal tax bracket or higher.

CAPITAL GAINS

A sound retirement plan requires dealing with the capital gain tax effectively. In spite of all of the tax legislation, real and proposed, capital gains remain an important element in your retirement planning. Naturally, however, the preferential capital gains tax rates apply only to nonretirement account assets.

Capital gains are the amounts that you realize whenever any capital asset such as stocks or bonds are sold at a profit. Conversely, a capital loss results when a capital asset is sold for an amount less than was paid for it. There are unique tax rates and rules that make both capital gains and losses quite rewarding from a tax standpoint.

 Unrealized Capital Gain. Gains on stock and property that you hold are not subject to income taxes. This is a major tax advantage and many investors have accumulated considerable wealth by buying and holding stocks and property. The value of these stocks and property rises over the years and yet there is no tax bill to pay.

Realized Capital Gain. When those stocks or property are sold at a gain—at a price that is higher than its cost—the amount of that gain is subject to federal income tax at capital gain tax rates.

Currently, the capital gain rates are the same as ordinary income tax rates, but they do not exceed 28 percent. Therefore, if you're in a higher tax bracket, you'll pay tax on capital gains at a rate that is lower than their marginal income tax rate.

Because unrealized gains are not taxed, you have complete control over the timing of when you will pay your taxes on those capital gains.

REALIZED CAPITAL LOSSES

Not all stock investments are winners. Inevitably, some will have to be sold at a loss. Fortunately, realized capital losses can be used to offset realized capital gains, which is often a smart move.

In addition to offsetting capital gains, up to $3,000 of excess capital losses may be utilized each year to offset other taxable income.

TAX BREAKS FOR SELLING YOUR RESIDENCE

When it comes to selling your principal residence, the tax laws offer two significant tax breaks to homeowners. The first is a one-time exclusion of up to $125,000 in capital gains on the sale of a primary residence. The second is more familiar: you can defer the taxes on your home-related capital gains by purchasing a more expensive residence.

Used together, these tax breaks can allow you to trade down (buy a less expensive home), pay less tax on the gain, and free up cash for your retirement.

BUYING DOWN AFTER 55

You can use the once-in-a-lifetime exclusion to help fund a portion of your retirement income needs using your equity in the home.

tip If you're 55 or older on the date of sale, you can use the once-in-a-lifetime exclusion rule to sell your primary residence and exclude up to $125,000 of profits from taxation. Any amount in excess of $125,000 is taxed as a capital gain.

! You qualify for the exclusion only if your home was your principal residence for at least three of the five years immediately prior to the sale. However, the house doesn't have to be your principal residence at the time it is sold. The IRS says that up to two years may pass between the time you vacate the house and the actual sale, as long as you lived in your house for three years before you vacated it.

You can make a really impressive tax-free maneuver by using both the $125,000 exclusion and the rollover-of-gain break. By combining these two provisions, you may collect more than $125,000 in profit and buy a home that costs as much as $125,000 less without paying a single penny in taxes.

If you paid $145,000 for your house in 1974, and 20 years later pay off the mortgage and sell it for $380,000 plus $20,000 in selling costs, you collect $215,000 profit. Because you're 56 years old (in this example), you sensibly opt to take the one-time exclusion—so $125,000 of your $215,000 gain would be tax free to you forever.

Now you want to purchase a new home. You may think you
have to find one of equal value to your old one so you'll
qualify for the rollover-of-gain break. However, when figuring
how much you must spend on a new home, the rules allow
you to subtract the amount of your exclusion ($125,000 from
the selling price of your old house ($380,000). So you must
spend only $255,000 for a new house—not $380,000.

As long as your new principal residence costs $255,000 or
more, you defer paying taxes on your remaining gain of
$90,000. You also reduce the basis or book value of your new
home by only the $90,000 gain that you don't pay taxes on
now. The $125,000 is excluded from taxes.

HOME EQUITY LOANS

When borrowing is necessary, your plan should be to find the
cheapest possible source of credit. For anyone who owns a
home with enough built-up equity, the least expensive credit
source is usually a home equity loan or line of credit.

To qualify for a unique tax break, the home equity loan must
be secured by your house. That means, of course, that your
home is on the line if you can't repay the loan.

In this lesson, you learned how to take advantage of tax rules
in your retirement planning. In the next lesson, you will learn
about the basic planning tools that can help catapult your
retirement savings nearer your retirement goals.

THE FOUNDATION OF YOUR RETIREMENT PLAN

In this lesson, you will learn that the foundation of your retirement plan consists of pensions, IRAs, and Keogh plans (for the self-employed).

PENSION PLANS

Your employer's pension plan is one of the most important tools in your retirement planning arsenal. The more generous the plan and the more effectively you tap its benefits, the more easily you can attain your retirement goals.

Every employer puts a different spin on its retirement benefits package. If you participate in several employers' plans over the course of your career, as is becoming more and more common, you may be entitled to collect from more than one plan.

HOW DOES YOUR EMPLOYER'S PLAN WORK?

Sizing up your own pension plan at work will give you the tools needed to fit this important piece into your overall retirement plan.

> *tip* If you and your spouse are employed by small companies that don't offer pension plans, don't panic. You're entitled to create your own tax-deductible, do-it-yourself pension plan with an individual retirement account (IRA). There are also other opportunities for the self-employed and small business owners to set aside funds on a tax-deferred basis.

SELF-DIRECTED PENSION PLANS

There has been a dramatic shift away from the traditional pension plans in which employers assume all responsibility for making contributions and managing the money. Now there are self-directed programs that make you take an active role on both counts.

For self-starters and those who want to be more involved in their own retirement plans, that shift is a major plus. You and your employer put money into an account with your name on it and you make decisions about where it is invested. Even better, if you leave your job, you can usually take the money with you.

MAKING THE MOST OF DEFINED BENEFIT PLANS

About 40 million Americans are covered by defined benefit plans.

> **Defined Benefit Plans.** Defined benefit plans guarantee to pay you a specified amount when you retire. This amount is based on your salary, age, and years of service. Defined benefit plans are backed by the government insurance agency called the Pension Benefit Guarantee Corporation (PBGC).

Most plans are designed so that the pension benefit plus Social Security benefits will replace 60 to 70 percent of an employee's preretirement income. This is a healthy sum when you consider that most retirement goals call for replacing 80 percent of that income.

To receive the maximum pension, most defined benefit plans require that you work at the company for 30 years and wait until "full retirement age"—that's usually age 62 or 65. Some companies use a point system that allows you to retire with full benefits once your age plus years of service total a certain number of points.

HOW DO YOU KNOW IF YOU'RE AN ACTIVE PARTICIPANT?

One of the easiest ways to find out whether you are an active participant is to look at your W-2 form. Frequently, these forms will indicate plan participation to the IRS where none actually exists. Your W-2 form includes a Pension Plan check box for your employer to check. If the box is checked, you know that you're an active participant in your employer's pension plan. If it's blank, you'd better know the active participation rules.

The IRS says that it makes no difference whether you actively participate in a defined benefit plan. It matters only that you're eligible to participate. Unfortunately, the rules are different for a defined contribution plan. Here you are considered an active participant if you or your company contribute money during the year to the plan on your behalf.

Remember, however, you are not an active participant if the only money that's added on your behalf during the year is earnings from the investments already in that plan.

DON'T OVERLOOK THAT GOVERNMENT PROTECTION

In a defined benefit plan, the employer is legally committed to making sure there's enough money in the plan to pay the guaranteed benefits. If the company fails to meet that obligation, the federal government will step in.

Defined benefit plans are the only type of pension insured by the Pension Benefit Guarantee Corporation (PBGC). The insurance works in much the same way that the Federal Deposit Insurance Corporation backs up your bank account.

If your plan is covered (most are), and the sponsoring company goes under, PBGC will take over benefit payments up to a set maximum (about $31,000 a year in 1995), which is adjusted periodically for inflation.

> **tip** This insurance protection helps make your pension more secure, but it is not a full guarantee that you'll get what you expect if the company you work for gets into trouble. Former employees of bankrupt companies, such as Pan Am and Eastern Airlines, saw their promised pensions reduced, and hundreds of other failed pension plans have been taken over by PBGC.

THOSE ALL-IMPORTANT INDIVIDUAL RETIREMENT ACCOUNTS

For those who have no way of participating in 401(k) plans or other self-directed, tax-deferred retirement plans (or if you have maximized your 401(k) savings), the next best place for your money may be an individual retirement account (IRA). IRAs may have lost some of their luster, but they can still be a key ingredient in your retirement plan.

Under current tax laws, if neither you nor your spouse participates in an employer-maintained retirement plan, you may contribute and deduct on your income tax return up to $2,000 for yourself and $2,000 for your spouse. If your spouse is not employed, then his or her contribution is reduced to $250.

If you or your spouse actively participates in an employer-maintained retirement plan, another set of rules applies. The IRS says that if you are single and an active participant, you may deduct your full contribution only if your adjusted gross income (AGI) is $25,000 or less. Your allowable deduction drops $10 for each $50 you earn above $25,000 until you reach $35,000, when the deduction phases out entirely.

If you're married and file jointly, and either one of you is an active participant, you get a full deduction only if your AGI is $40,000 or less. Your deduction drops by $10 for each $50 in income up to $50,000, where the deduction vanishes. Filing separately won't help. If married couples file separately, no tax deduction is allowable to either person.

How many IRAs can you have? The IRS doesn't care if you set up one IRA or a dozen. You may set them up at as many financial institutions as you want. However, be careful when you open multiple accounts. Most institutions charge you annual fees—up to $50 or more—to maintain your IRA. So, if you maintain many small accounts and they all charge fees, your investment return effectively drops.

tip   You're allowed to deduct the annual maintenance fee as a miscellaneous itemized deduction. But you may write it off only if you pay it out of separate funds, and it and all other miscellaneous itemized deductions exceed two percent of your adjusted gross income.

INVESTING IN AN IRA

The trustee of your IRA may be the institution or institutions where you maintain your IRA: such as a bank, savings and loan, mutual fund, and so on. Or, you may manage your account yourself and invest as you see fit. If the latter is your choice, you would use a bank or brokerage house as custodian of your IRA.

You can invest your IRA in most regular investment vehicles: CDs, mutual funds, stocks, or bonds, for example.

> **tip**
> You don't have total freedom when it comes to investing your IRA dollars. You can buy an annuity but you can't buy a life insurance contract. Art objects, antiques, gold or silver coins (except gold and silver coins minted by the United States), stamps, and other collectibles are also not permitted when it comes to IRA investing.

If you do use IRA dollars for prohibited investments, Uncle Sam treats the current year investment as a withdrawal from your account. That means you must pay tax on that amount at ordinary tax rates and, if you invest in the item before age 59 and a half, you must pay an additional 10 percent penalty.

> **!**
> There's one more investment you should avoid when it comes to your IRA: municipal bonds or other tax-free investments. As you know, the money in your IRA account is taxed when you withdraw it. Municipal bonds are tax-free. So, by putting those bonds in your IRA, you're converting tax-free income into taxable income.

USING A KEOGH PLAN

The basic retirement program for self-employed individuals is called a Keogh plan. It's named after Daniel Keogh, the Congressman whose legislation authorized the tax break that makes the plan so popular.

 **Keogh Plan.** A Keogh plan is a type of retirement plan for self-employed people. Contributions are fully tax deductible. The plan also serves as a tax shelter: there's no tax on earnings until you withdraw the money, presumably in retirement.

Contributions to your personal pension plan are always fully tax deductible, no matter how high your income and regardless of whether you or your spouse are covered by another retirement plan. There's no such thing as a nondeductible contribution as there is with an IRA.

In fact, you can have an IRA in addition to your Keogh. Of course, whether IRA contributions would be deductible depends on your income, because a Keogh is considered an employer-sponsored plan for purposes of IRA deductibility tests.

How much can you contribute? That depends on how much self-employment income you have and what kind of Keogh plan you choose. The limits generally range from 15 percent to 25 percent of your self-employment earnings to a maximum of $22,500 to $30,000 per year.

There is one major drawback to having your own small business pension plan: if you have employees, they must be included in the plan and you must contribute roughly the same percentage of income to their accounts as you contribute to your own.

SIMPLIFIED EMPLOYEE PENSION PLANS

There is an alternative to the Keogh plan; it's known as the simplified employee pension (SEP).

Simplified Employee Pension. SEP is a low-cost, low maintenance plan, a so-called "business IRA," that permits a fully tax-deductible contribution far above the $2,000 limit for individual IRAs.

It's easy to set up a SEP; it requires far less paperwork than a Keogh or other small business pension plans. Just like the complex pension programs offered by big corporations, SEPs deliver important tax savings to both employers and employees.

Your business or self-employment taxable income is reduced by the amount of money you put into your SEP. The money in your plan, including earnings on investments, grows untouched until you withdraw it.

Virtually anyone with income from self-employment is eligible to open a SEP: sole proprietors, partners, owners of corporations or S corporations, even freelancers and moonlighters. Whether you earn a few dollars selling crafts on weekends or you're a founding partner in a high-powered consulting firm, you qualify for a SEP.

A SEP is a cross between a profit-sharing Keogh plan and an IRA. Your contributions go into a special SEP-IRA. You can contribute as much as 15 percent of your net self-employment earnings, up to a maximum of $22,500.

In this lesson, you learned about company pensions, IRAs, and retirement accounts for the self-employed. These should form the foundation of your retirement plan. In the next lesson, you will learn how to build your retirement portfolio by taking advantage of 401(k) plans and other employer-sponsored benefit plans.

BUILD YOUR RETIREMENT FUNDS ON COMPANY TIME

In this lesson, you will learn how to take full advantage of your employer benefit plans to reach your financial goals.

EMPLOYEE SAVINGS PLANS

Probably the most popular retirement benefit plan is the 401(k) plan, which is named for the IRS regulation governing it.

> **401(k) Plan.** A 401(k) plan is an employer savings plan that lets you set aside a percentage of your salary, currently up to $9,240, in a tax-deferred account.

You pay no federal or state (except in Pennsylvania) taxes on the dollars you contribute to your 401(k) plan until you withdraw them, usually at retirement. Your interest, dividends, and other earnings in the plan accumulate tax-deferred until withdrawal. The real advantage of the plan is that many employers match your contribution, usually by 50 percent.

The maximum amount you can contribute is indexed to inflation, but is adjusted upward only when the cumulative growth in the consumer price index is large enough to cause the deferred limit to increase by $500.

There are many reasons why you should participate in a 401(k) plan:

- To reduce your current tax bill.

- To accumulate retirement savings on a tax-deferred basis.

- To pay yourself first. This is the "forced savings" aspect—you pay yourself first and never see the money.

- To get an automatic return on your money—often as much as 50 percent—through the matching contributions of your employer.

Many 401(k) plans allow you to borrow your funds at reasonable interest rates, although you'll have a taxable distribution if you leave the company without paying the loan back.

MATCHING MEANS MORE

Many employers match the amount that employees put away in their plans. Your employer might, for instance, contribute 50 cents for every dollar you set aside (up to limits specified in the plan). Employers usually cap their contributions to the first three to six percent of your wages that you contribute.

For many employees, a key reason for participating in an employer-sponsored 401(k) savings plan is to collect the matching contributions from the company.

tip You may not own those matching funds immediately: that portion of the contribution is usually subject to a vesting schedule. With a vesting schedule, the employee takes ownership of the contribution over a period of time. The period of time is usually based on your length of service, and it can't be longer than seven years (five years is considered the standard).

401(K) LIMITS

Not too surprisingly, there are limits on the amount you can contribute to a 401(k) plan. The IRS sets several ceilings on 401(k) contributions, including the most important two:

- You may put aside a percentage of your wages (the percentage allowed depends on your company's plan) as a pretax contribution into a 401(k) plan, but this contribution can't be more than $9,240 (in 1995). Many employers also allow 401(k) contributions to be taken out of bonuses.

- The maximum salary that can be used to figure your contribution to a 401(k) plan is $150,000. This amount is adjusted annually for inflation.

401(K) INVESTMENT OPTIONS

Under federal law, a 401(k) plan must allow you to choose among at least three investment options. These investments often include equity mutual funds, shares of stock in your company, money market accounts, guaranteed investment contracts (GICs), and government securities (such as Treasury bills).

> *tip* Under recently issued U.S. Department of Labor rules, companies will be able to minimize their exposure to investment-related claims by providing you with detailed information so you understand the choices available to you and the risk associated with each option.

EMPLOYEE SAVINGS PLANS (NONPROFITS)

If you work for a nonprofit organization, such as a hospital, university, or public school, you are eligible for something similar to the 401(k) plans of private industry: a 403(b) plan. These nonprofit plans include:

- A section 403(b) plan (commonly called a tax-deferred annuity plan) for employees of colleges, universities, and nonprofit organizations.

- A section 457 plan for employees of colleges, universities, and local government entities.

Your employer may sponsor a 403(b) or, if not, you may be able to arrange for an individual 403(b) plan through an insurance company or mutual fund. As with a 401(k) plan, your salary is reduced by the amount of your contribution to a 403(b) plan.

The annual contribution limit is 25 percent of your salary up to a ceiling of $9,500. That ceiling will be adjusted upward for inflation once the 401(k) ceiling (current $9,240) catches up with it.

TAX-DEFERRED ISN'T TAX-FREE

Obviously, tax-deferred isn't the same as tax-free. The money you put away is taxable to you when you withdraw it, so you won't escape taxes entirely. You simply postpone them until you withdraw your money.

If you and your spouse can contribute in pretax dollars and allow those dollars to grow tax-deferred, you have the best of all worlds. Even if only your earnings are tax-deferred, you're still likely to build you retirement nest egg faster. In fact, as you'll see when you explore tax deferred and tax-free investment vehicles in more depth in Lesson 14, there is an order of investments you should consider to maximize the return on your retirement savings.

COMPANY HELP WITH YOUR RETIREMENT PLAN

You want to take full advantage of any tax-deferred plans that your employer offers. If you can, for example, participate in a 401(k) plan, sign up at the first chance, and put in the most you can possible afford. Not only will you defer taxes on current income, you will also defer taxes on the earnings. Hopefully, you may even benefit from matching contributions from your employer.

AFTER THE 401(K) PLAN

After taking full advantage of the 401(k) plan offered by your employer, the next step is to make after-tax contributions to your 401(k). Not all plans allow after-tax contributions, but if yours does, it's similar to making a nondeductible IRA contribution without the $2,000 limitation.

tip Your after-tax contributions will, however, be limited by the percent limits on your 401(k) plan. Even though you might not be able to get a tax deduction for the annual contribution, the earnings grow tax-deferred. As you have seen, that can be worth a lot.

EMPLOYEE THRIFT AND SAVINGS PLANS

These usually require after-tax contributions that are either wholly or partially matched by the employer's contributions. Even though there are no immediate tax benefits, you get something for nothing (your employer's contribution) and your savings will benefit from accumulating tax-deferred.

PROFIT SHARING PLANS

If one is available, you should participate in your company's profit sharing plan.

Profit Sharing Plan. A profit sharing plan allows employees to share in company profits, usually based on a percentage of their salary.

Under current laws, a company may make contributions to a profit sharing plan even if it reports no earnings. Also it may change the amount of contributions from one year to the next.

Normally, profit-sharing contributions are allocated to employee accounts in proportion to their current salary. The company—not you—decides how the money in the plan is invested.

Here the company takes the lead with annual contributions based on the firm's profitability. You may or may not have the option of contributing to the plan yourself.

Profit sharing plans have a number of benefits:

- If the company does well, the profit sharing arrangement lets you participate in that success.

- A company that grows wildly could net you a sizable retirement nest egg.

- If a portion of the money in this plan is invested in stocks, you have another important tool for beating inflation.

A drawback is that the ultimate size of your nest egg is not entirely predictable with a profit sharing plan because the size of the contributions can vary from year to year.

EMPLOYEE STOCK OWNERSHIP PLANS

Employee stock ownership plans (ESOPs) are one type of profit sharing arrangement.

 ESOP. In ESOP plans, the employer contributes shares of company stock to your retirement arrangement, or lets you buy shares as a plan investment option.

An ESOP is a way to acquire stock in the firm you work for at little or no commission cost or even at a share price discount. You'll pay taxes on the value of the shares only when you take possession or leave the company. In the meantime, the stock can appreciate tax-free.

In this lesson, you learned how to fully utilize your employer benefit plans to reach your financial goals. In the next lesson, you will learn about cash and cash equivalent investments.

INVESTING CASH RESERVES

In this lesson, you will learn about cash and cash equivalent investments that play a significant role in retirement planning.

HOW TO HAVE A STEADY INCOME BEFORE AND AFTER RETIREMENT

Older investors and retirees look to cash and cash equivalent investments to provide steady, predictable income streams while maintaining safety of principal.

Cash Equivalent Investments. Cash equivalent investments are issued by borrowers (such as government agencies, large corporations, and banks) with strong financial positions.

Principal. The face value of an obligation that must be repaid at maturity as separate from the interest.

Interest. The cost of using someone else's money. It can also be defined as income derived from a bank account or investment.

If interest rates plunge, the return on your cash investments can drop to very low levels. Naturally, you pay a price for safety and liquidity in the form of lower yields. Historically, cash and cash equivalent investments have provided yields that have barely exceeded the annual rate of inflation.

Because of these yields there are two reasons for anyone over 40 (but not yet retired) who is planning their retirement to invest in cash equivalents: To maintain a reserve for emergencies and as a short-term, low-risk place to put funds awaiting investment in other vehicles.

Yield. The return on an investor's capital investment.

INTRODUCTION TO INVESTING

Retirement planning means investing. As an investor, you pay cash now in return for cash to be received at a future date. This can take the form of either savings or investing.

SAVINGS

With savings, you put an amount of money in a savings account or in a cash equivalent, such as money market accounts, Treasury bills, or CDs. The amount saved usually earns interest. At the end of the period, you withdraw the funds that were originally deposited along with any interest they earned while entrusted to the bank, broker, or government.

INVESTMENTS

An investment involves risking your money in exchange for the possibility that those savings will increase before you need them. Investments may pay interest or dividends as well as offer opportunities for the growth of your capital.

CASH EQUIVALENTS

Cash equivalents are short-term, interest-earning securities that can be readily converted into cash with little or no change in principal value.

Cash equivalents provide a reliable home for money that might be needed in a relatively short time. While they are liquid and relatively safe, cash equivalents have not historically provided much in the way of investment returns. Over most periods, their returns have generally been about the same as the rate of inflation. They offer the advantages of liquidity and stability of principal because of their high credit quality and short maturities.

Treasury bills, for example, are offered at maturities of one year or less. Commercial paper, a debt obligation issued by top-rated corporations, typically has a maturity of 90 days or less.

The financial strength of most borrowers in the market for cash equivalents (such as government agencies, large corporations, and banks) combined with the short maturity of cash reserve investments means that cash equivalents are essentially immune from significant market risk and interest rate risk.

> ***tip*** The preservation of capital is extremely important if you're over the age of 40. It's important that you preserve your capital because you don't have the time to make up or replace money lost with more risky savings or investments.

Cash equivalent investments include the following: money market accounts, money market funds, savings accounts, Certificates of deposit (CDs), and Treasury bills.

Cash equivalent investments provide stability of principal and offer interest rates that change periodically. The interest paid on cash equivalent investments fluctuates when other interest rates drop. This can prove troublesome to anyone over 40 who's attempting to plan their retirement income.

> ***tip*** Because the interest rates on cash equivalents are generally close to the inflation rate for the same period, they are best viewed as a temporary parking place for your money while you are awaiting a more attractive investment opportunity.

MONEY MARKET ACCOUNTS AND FUNDS

Don't confuse the money market accounts that are offered by banks and Savings and Loan Associations (S&Ls) with money market funds offered by brokerage and mutual fund companies. Think of money market accounts as limited checking accounts (you can write only a few checks each month in most cases) that pay daily interest in relation to market rates. Because they're offered by banks and S&Ls, money market accounts carry Federal Deposit Insurance Corporation (FDIC) insurance up to $100,000 and are, thus, generally risk-free.

Money market funds are not insured by any government agency. That should not cause much concern. After all, money market funds invest in the highest quality U.S. government securities, commercial paper, banker's acceptances, and other securities. Money market funds usually pay a higher rate of interest than bank money market accounts.

SAVINGS ACCOUNTS

If you save $200 per month in a basic savings account at your local bank for 20 years, earning five percent annually, your total when you reach age 65 will be $82,560 (without accounting for taxes). That includes $48,000 of principal that you invested plus $34,560 in earnings for that money.

> **!** If you're over 40 already, you don't have 30 years before retirement. It is imperative that you increase the yield or return on your savings or investments that you make.

CDs

Banks and savings institutions may offer certificates of deposit (CDs) at whatever amount, maturity, and interest rate they choose. This means that you can shop among banks to find the CD package that is best for your retirement plan.

> ***tip*** Because you can buy and redeem CDs by mail, it's just as easy to do business with a bank in another state as with one across the street. You can also purchase CDs from brokerage firms. You'll pay a brokerage fee, of course, but brokerage firms often pay a higher rate of interest.

When investing in CDs, you should be aware of the following:

- If the interest rate a bank offers is substantially higher than the going rate for CDs of similar amount and maturity, be skeptical. The bank may be in a shabby financial condition and forced to offer the higher rate to attract new money.

- If the bank is an FDIC institution, FDIC insurance would cover your loss if the bank went belly-up—but not necessarily the interest due you, not to mention having the money tied up for months.

With CDs, you might also find out about getting your money back before the CD matures. In some cases, the bank or S&L can penalize you with an early withdrawal penalty that can wipe out any interest due you.

WHERE DO YOU BUY TREASURY BILLS?

You can purchase Treasury bills through a broker or a bank in denominations of $10,000 or higher, and thereafter in multiples of $5,000. When buying Treasury bills, remember the following points:

- Brokers and banks usually charge small fees, usually $25 to $50 per transaction.

- You can purchase Treasury bills in a variety of maturities: 90 days, 180 days, or 52 weeks.

- You can eliminate commission charges by buying Treasury bills directly from Federal Reserve banks or their branches.

tip You can receive a free brochure on how to buy Treasury securities from a Federal Reserve bank or branch by writing to:

Bureau of Public Debt
Division of Customer Service
300 13th Street SW
Washington, DC 20239-0001

In this lesson, you learned about several good, low-risk, short-term investments. In the next lesson, you will learn about the growth investments that will form the basis of your self-invested retirement planning portfolio.

Growth Investments for Your Retirement Portfolio

In this lesson, you will learn about growth investments, including stocks and bonds, that should be a part of your retirement portfolio.

A Divided Portfolio for Growth—and Safety

You have learned in earlier lessons that your retirement portfolio should be divided among a variety of investments. The growth portion of your portfolio should include both growth stocks and growth-oriented mutual funds.

Selecting growth in both individual stocks and in mutual funds means seeking companies that will generate above-average increases in earnings, and will outperform the market in the long run.

STOCKS

Usually when you buy a stock, you are buying common stock. Common stock may or may not pay dividends. The amount of dividends that each share of stock pays is known as the yield. If some shares of stock pay relatively small dividends, a higher yield might be obtained by simply investing those funds in Treasury bills. By the same token, if the choice has to be made between the stock of two companies within the same industry, both with comparable qualities, the amount of the dividend may be an important deciding factor.

Stock. The term "stock" usually refers to common stock, which represents an ownership share in the company that issued it.

Dividends. Dividends are profits that the company distributes to its owners and shareholders.

Yield. Yield is determined by dividing the current annual dividend of any stock by the share price.

Many companies also issue a special class of shares called "preferred" stock. These shares generally pay a higher dividend than common stock but don't have the same price-appreciation potential of common stock.

CATEGORIES OF STOCKS

Although thousands of companies issue shares of stock, most of those shares fall into the categories of common, preferred, or restricted stock. In general, however, most stock is categorized by the type of return it offers.

There are five basic, often overlapping, stock categories that you should consider for your own retirement portfolio:

- **Growth Stocks.** These stocks have good prospects for growing faster than the economy or the stock market in general. Investors like them for their consistent earnings growth and the likelihood that share prices will go up significantly over the long-term.

- **Blue Chip Stocks.** This is another loosely defined group. Many large growth stocks are often also considered blue chip. Blue chip stocks are generally shares of stock in industry-leading companies with highly rated financial credentials. They tend to pay decent, steadily rising dividends, generate some growth, and offer safety and reliability.

  Blue chip stocks should form your retirement portfolio's core holding, which is a group of stocks you plan to hold forever while adding to your position as your portfolio grows.

- **Income Stocks.** These securities pay a much larger portion of their profits, often as much as 50 to 80 percent, to investors in the form of quarterly dividends than do other stocks. These tend to be more mature, slower-growth companies and the dividends paid to investors make these shares generally less risky to own than shares of growth or small company stocks.

tip Though share prices of income stocks aren't expected to grow rapidly, the dividend acts as a kind of cushion beneath the share price. Even if the market in general falls, income stocks are usually less affected because investors will still receive the dividend.

tip Dividends are only one way that income stocks make money for your retirement nest egg. The key is their total return: the combination of dividends plus the growth in the price of the shares.

- **Small Company Stocks.** Shares in these companies are riskier than blue chip or income stocks. But, as a group, their long-term average returns are also higher. These are typically newer, fast-growing companies.

- **Foreign Stocks.** These investments also play a role in most retirement nest eggs. They're available through an array of foreign stock mutual funds. The two key benefits of adding an international flavor to your nest egg are diversification and performance.

While most investors think only in terms of owning U.S. shares, the American market represents less than half of all stock market opportunities worldwide. Foreign shares help diversify your nest egg because international markets usually perform differently than the U.S. market does. When stocks in the U.S. are down, those in other countries may be rising.

> ❗ Because of the currency risk of owning foreign stocks, most small investors are better off in an international mutual fund that spreads this risk among many countries and currencies.

STOCKS AND LONG-TERM GAINS

Stocks are the best place to invest your retirement nest egg, even if you're planning to retire in less than 10 years. In the long-term performance race, stocks are winners by a big margin over virtually any time period chosen.

Since 1926, a basket of blue chip stocks has shown an average annual gain of 10.4 percent. Small company stocks, which tend to grow faster but with more risk, have produced an average annual gain of more than 12 percent since the 1920s (according to the literature put out by the American Stock Exchange and several brokerage houses).

STOCK INVESTING TIPS

Tips on the stock market are as common—and about as reliable—as tips on horse races. Over the years, however, investors have developed strategies and techniques for investing in the stock market. Even if you're not trying to be a Wall Street expert, you'll be better able to pick stocks if you understand some basic stock buying and selling strategies.

Remember the following:

- Never buy stocks indiscriminately; make investments only when you have a reason to buy them.

- Select a promising industry, one with a good future outlook.

- Diversify. Try to own stocks in several industries.

- Buy low and sell high. This sounds easy but it's difficult to achieve.

- Stay abreast of market trends.

- Use stop-loss orders to protect against losses. Stop-loss orders fence in gains by restricting the effects of a market downturn on your stocks.

- Buy value. Companies with strong finances (not too much debt) and solid earnings growth are consistently better long-term purchases.

MUTUAL FUNDS: LET SOMEONE ELSE PICK YOUR STOCKS

There is an alternative to buying individual stocks. You can put your money into a stock mutual fund.

Mutual Fund. A mutual fund is a professionally managed investment company comprised of a pool of investors' money used to purchase a diversified portfolio of stocks, bonds, money market instruments, or other securities. Each share in a mutual fund represents a small slice of the mutual fund's total portfolio.

Mutual funds grew from just over $100 billion in assets in 1980 to more than $1.6 trillion in assets by 1993. The result is that, today, there are more than 3,400 mutual funds to choose from compared to about 500 just a decade ago.

Why are mutual funds such a popular way to invest? There are several reasons:

- It's easy to invest in them. You can purchase shares in a mutual fund often with a modest initial amount of $50 or $100. Transactions can be done by phone.

- Probably the most significant explanation for mutual funds' popularity is their performance. The average stock mutual fund's annual rate of return over the past decade was almost 12 percent.

- Funds are a low-cost way to diversify your retirement investments, thereby reducing investment risk.

- Funds are managed by experienced professionals who are responsible for investing and managing the stock and/or bond holdings continuously.

- Another option with mutual funds is that many automatically reinvest dividends and capital gains.

- Planned investment programs are also offered and listed in newspapers, which makes it easy to keep tabs on performance.

There are some disadvantages:

- Like the securities that they invest in, a mutual fund's asset value will fluctuate with changing market conditions.

- Commission and fee structures of mutual funds can be confusing.

The funds range from no-load funds (which carry no sales commissions and are sold only to the public) to low-load funds (which have a commission of one to three percent) to load funds (which typically charge commissions of four to eight and a half percent)

MUTUAL FUND CATEGORIES

Like stocks, mutual funds also fall into a number of very broad categories.

- **Stock Fund.** A stock (or equity) mutual fund invests its money in stocks of individual companies, large and small, new and old, here and abroad.

- **Bond Funds.** A bond mutual fund invests its money in bonds of companies or governments that are as varied as those that stock funds invest in.

- **Money Market Funds.** A money market fund invests its money in short-term financial instruments, such as Treasury bills and CDs.

Mutual funds types are often described as:

- **Open-End Mutual Funds.** These sell an unlimited number of new shares and constantly repurchase or redeem outstanding ones. So, the amount of money in the fund is always changing.

- **Closed-End Mutual Funds.** These have a relatively fixed amount of assets under management. Closed-end funds raise money as ordinary companies do—with an initial offering on a recognized stock exchange. After they're issued, the shares of closed-end mutual funds are traded just like any other stock: on the major stock exchanges and over the counter.

MUTUAL FUND SAFETY

While mutual funds are not insured or guaranteed by any government agency, their operations are regulated by the U.S. Securities and Exchange Commission and by state agencies. The Investment Company Act of 1940, the principal federal law regulating mutual funds, requires funds to operate in the interest of shareholders and to take steps to safeguard their assets.

MUTUAL FUND TAX STRATEGY

With 10 years or so to go before your retirement, it's important that you invest prudently for maximum return. Spreading the risk or compensating for your lack of knowledge of stocks can be accomplished by using mutual funds.

If you are investing through a taxable investment account, put the emphasis on low-yielding growth funds rather than higher-yielding funds. Doing this will minimize your current taxable dividend income.

As you change your portfolio allocation over time, try to minimize the extent of capital gains realization from the re-balancing. It is always more tax-effective to adjust your asset allocation by adding new contributions to a lagging investment rather than selling an appreciated investment. Naturally, this is not relevant in a retirement account because all income and capital gains will be tax deferred.

In this lesson, you learned about the role that stocks and stock mutual funds play in your retirement portfolio. In the next lesson, you will learn about investing for income.

INCOME INVESTMENTS

In this lesson, you will learn why income-producing investments, which exceed interest on bank products, should be part of your retirement portfolio.

THE ROLE OF CASH AND INCOME INVESTMENTS

Cash and fixed-income investments play an important role in any portfolio, whether you're 25 years from retirement or already retired. If you're over age 40, you usually will invest in cash and bonds to provide a stable level of income and to reduce the overall level of risk in your portfolio. This will break down to perhaps up to 20 percent between the ages of 40 and 60; for those over 60, perhaps 40 to 60 percent.

INCOME FROM BONDS

Bonds are called fixed-income securities because the interest they pay, known as the coupon, is typically a fixed amount. A $1,000 bond issued with a seven percent coupon would pay a fixed $70 in interest each year.

Bond. A bond is a loan in the form of a publicly traded security. An investor who buys a bond is making a loan for a certain number of years to the government agency, corporation, or other entity that issues the bond.

While the coupon amount of the bond may be fixed, the price of the bond is not. A bond may agree to pay seven percent interest on its face value. Investors, on the other hand, may price that bond and its seven percent return at a fraction of its face value. Holding the bond to maturity will ensure a profit over the amount paid and, in the meantime, a rate of return higher than the seven percent offered will be yours to reinvest.

As interest rates rise, bond prices will drop; falling interest rates cause bond prices to move upward. Investors will bid up or push down a bond's price until its yield to maturity is in line with market interest rates.

WHY INVEST IN BONDS?

There are several reasons why bonds are attractive to investors who plan to retire in ten years or less or to people who need a stream of income:

- They provide higher income than cash equivalents (such as Treasury bills or money market funds). Accordingly, many investors, such as retired individuals who require current income to meet their living expenses, allocate the bulk of their investment portfolio to bonds.

- Bond income is also highly predictable. If you purchase a government bond, you are assured of receiving payments of interest and principal when they come due. Thus, bonds can be used to fund future obligations.

* Bonds provide portfolio diversification, which can help dampen the effects of swings in stock prices. This is because bond prices, in general, do not correlate to the movement of stock prices. They are usually less volatile than stocks.

Should you be concerned about fluctuations in bond prices? Not if your intent is to hold bond investments until they mature. Unlike stocks, bonds have a maturity date at which point the bond issuer will return the principal at par value. In the meantime, swings in interest rates may cause your bond's price to rise above or fall below par, but you don't need to worry.

Par Value. Stated or face value of a stock or bond. The par value of bonds specifies the payment at maturity.

You can be assured of getting your money back as long as the bond issuer is creditworthy.

This applies to individual bonds but not to bond market funds because mutual funds do not have a particular maturity date when principal is returned.

GOVERNMENT BONDS

Certain government agencies also issue securities. Some of the bonds are explicitly guaranteed by the U.S. government, but all are considered safe because even without an express guarantee, the risk of default is considered extremely low.

The best known are mortgage pools: pools of home mortgages issued by the Government National Mortgage Association (GNMA or Ginnie Mae), Federal National Mortgage Association (FNMA or Fannie Mae), and Federal Home Loan Mortgage Corporation (FHLMC or Freddie Mac). These entities all buy mortgages from banks and thrifts, pool them, and then sell units of the pools to investors.

GINNIE MAES

When you buy Ginnie Maes, you are actually purchasing a portion of the 30-year mortgages issued by the U.S. Federal Housing Administration (FHA) and the Veterans Administration (VA). Ginnie Mae collects monthly interest and principal payments that homeowners pay on their mortgages, subtracts a small administrative fee, and passes the payments on to its investors.

Because homeowners' monthly payments include principal and interest, the check that investors receive each month includes both interest income and some principal. Only the interest portion, of course, is taxable. The amount of principal and interest a Ginnie Mae pays each month fluctuates because some homeowners pay off their mortgages (they sell or refinance their homes). So, if you invest in Ginnie Maes, you can't predict precisely how much you'll receive each month.

tip   It is this prepayment risk that causes Ginnie Maes—although they are government backed—to pay a rate of return higher than those available on U.S. Treasury bonds. Before you make a Ginnie Mae investment, you should decide whether the additional premium is large enough to offset the additional risk.

FANNIE MAES AND FREDDIE MACS

Fannie Maes and Freddie Macs are two other types of mortgage-backed securities. These securities make regular interest payments but you don't receive your principal until the securities mature.

Fannie Maes and Freddie Macs carry more risk than Ginnie Maes because they invest in mortgages that aren't insured by the FHA or VA. Even though the mortgage isn't guaranteed, the FNMA and the FHLMC do guarantee that you will receive your interest payments. Because these securities are riskier, they can pay a higher rate of interest than a Ginnie Mae.

Mortgage-backed securities pay a better yield than other government securities and you don't give up much in safety. Not only are these securities backed by the government, they're also collateralized by the real estate they finance.

BUYING TREASURY SECURITIES

Treasury securities are the means by which the U.S. government borrows money. Treasury bills, notes, and bonds are issued regularly by the Federal Reserve and are a popular investment for people who want very little default risk. Naturally, they are subject to purchasing power risk; notes and bonds are subject to interest rate risk.

tip   Because these are direct obligations of the U.S. government, the interest on Treasury bills, notes, and bonds is usually exempt from state income taxes.

Treasury bills are cash-equivalent debt instruments issued at various maturities. Auctions of 90-day and the 182-day bills take place weekly. The Treasury also auctions 52-week bills once every four weeks.

Treasury bills are issued in minimum denominations of $10,000, and subsequent purchases may be made at $5,000 increments. Treasury bills are sold at a discount from the face (maturity) value. The amount of that discount is equal to the interest that will be paid at maturity. Therefore, upon maturity, the investor receives the face value of the Treasury bill.

Treasury notes and bonds are fixed-income obligations that have longer terms and pay interest semiannually at a fixed interest rate. They are sold at face value.

ZERO COUPON BONDS

An interesting type of U.S. Treasury security is the zero coupon bond. These bonds pay no interest between the time they are purchased and the time that they are sold. Instead, they are sold at a deep discount or at a price that is much lower than the maturity value of the bond.

Because you don't get any interest during the holding period, your profit comes at maturity in the form of a large increase in the amount you receive.

The main advantage of zero coupon bonds is that you are guaranteed a set return at the original interest rates. Therefore, if interest rates decline, you don't have to worry about reinvesting interest income at a lower rate. This automatic compounding also avoids your having to decide on reinvesting the interest you would receive on a regular bond. Naturally, they are still subject to purchasing power risk.

> **!** Even though you are not receiving interest along the way, the IRS assumes you are for income tax purposes. So you have to pay income taxes on that imputed interest income in a nonretirement account.

CORPORATE BONDS

Corporate bonds are somewhat riskier than bonds issued by the U.S. government. If the company issuing your bond goes belly-up, your ability to get your money back depends on the provisions of the bond you buy.

Most corporations issue bonds in denominations of $1,000, but you must buy them in lots of five. You can, however, invest in a bond mutual fund, where the initial investment requirements can be as low as $250. By investing in a bond mutual fund, you'll have a very diversified bond portfolio because you'll own a share of probably 50 to 100 different bonds.

The interest that you earn on corporate bonds is subject to federal, state, and local taxes. Corporate bonds are liquid. You can usually sell them without too much trouble before they mature. Bonds that carry the highest ratings are the most liquid.

Corporate bonds should be a part of your retirement portfolio because of their return—higher than treasury securities—and relative safety of the principal.

ARE HIGH-YIELD BONDS REALLY "JUNK?"

A high-yield bond is a unique type of corporate bond known in the trade as a "junk bond." These investments pay very high yields and for a good reason: the risk you take when you purchase the bond is very high because of its poor credit rating.

Junk Bond. A bond with a speculative credit rating. Junk bonds are usually issued in leveraged buyouts, or other forms of corporate takeovers, by companies without long track records of sales and earnings or by those with questionable credit strength.

If the company goes belly-up, you'll probably lose every penny you invest. Recently, defaults on these low-grade corporate bonds occurred more frequently than defaults on other corporate bonds. The outlook for these bonds is uncertain, so you should probably avoid them.

tip One way to reduce the impact of interest rate changes in the value of a portfolio of individual bonds is to "ladder" maturities, which means to hold a mix of short-, intermediate-, and long-term bonds.

In this lesson, you learned about income investments and how they can provide stability to your portfolio as you approach retirement. In the next lesson, you will learn about other types of income investments that offer tax advantages.

TAX-FREE AND TAX-DEFERRED INCOME INVESTMENTS

In this lesson, you will learn about the role that tax-exempt, tax-deferred, and tax-free investments play in helping people over 40 achieve their retirement goals.

THE ROLE OF TAX-EXEMPT INVESTMENTS

Obviously, when you can select an investment on which you'll owe no taxes, you should do so. This type of security is known as a tax-exempt bond, stock, or investment.

Tax-Exempt Security. A tax-exempt security is an obligation whose interest is exempt from taxation by federal, state, and/or local authorities. It is frequently called a municipal bond even though it may have been issued by a state government or agency.

There's a quick rule of thumb about when to consider investing in tax-free securities, if your taxable income is expected to place you in the 28 percent tax bracket or higher. With few exceptions, interest received on municipal investments is exempt from all federal income taxes and, in some cases, from state and local taxes. High federal and state taxes result in many investors considering the benefits of investing in municipal bonds.

Municipal Securities

Municipal securities, often referred to as "munis," are debt obligations that have been issued by state and local governments and governmental agencies, such as highway departments, an airport authority, a school district, even a sewer commission.

 Debt Obligation. Debt obligations are interest-paying IOUs that raise money for a variety of state or local government purposes.

State and local governments issue debt obligations for a variety of reasons, which gives you many options to choose from. Keep in mind: the interest on most municipals is usually exempt from federal taxes. That interest is exempt from state and local taxes if you are a resident of the state that issues the debt.

! One risk of using either individual municipal bonds or shares in a municipal bond fund is that if interest rates rise, the value of the securities may decline. This is known as interest rate risk.

If interest rates decline, the value of the municipal bonds or the share price of a municipal bond fund investment may increase.

Capital Gains Taxes

Capital gains that may be realized when a municipal security is sold will be subject to federal and most state capital gains taxes.

> **!** Sometimes the managers of a bond fund may sell some securities at a gain. These realized capital gains are taxable to the fund shareholders, who may have to pay a capital gains tax even though they haven't yet sold their shares in the fund.

Double Tax-Free Securities

Investors who hold municipal securities of issuers located within their own state get a double benefit: interest on these bonds or notes is free from both federal and state taxes.

Tax-Exempt Funds

If you're in the highest tax brackets, the potentially higher after-tax yields of municipal money market funds and municipal bond funds may make them appropriate alternatives to taxable funds. Municipal funds typically pay lower pretax yields than taxable funds, but their tax adjusted yields should be superior for high tax bracket investors.

Interest income from municipal bond funds is generally exempt from federal income taxes. In addition, if a fund invests primarily in the debt obligations of the state in which you reside, the fund's dividend income will be exempt from state and local taxes as well.

Some municipal bond funds also generate "tax preference" items, which may affect high income taxpayers who are subject to the Federal Alternative Minimum Tax (AMT).

Alternative Minimum Tax. The AMT is a flat tax to ensure that high income individuals pay at least some tax, regardless of their deductions.

You should remember that, while dividend income from municipal funds escapes federal taxation, capital gains distributions do not. They are fully taxable at the federal level and may be subject to state and local taxes as well.

U.S. TREASURY SECURITIES

One final tax exemption worth noting applies to funds that invest in U.S. Treasury securities. All income derived from U.S. Treasury obligations is exempt from state and local taxes in every state. Unfortunately, federal income taxes still apply to U.S. Treasury income, but the high income taxes of many states may make these funds worth investigating.

TAX-DEFERRED INVESTMENTS

The IRS looks favorably upon working people who set aside money for retirement via 401(k) plans, 403(b) plans, IRAs, and so on, by allowing such savings to grow free of tax until the money is withdrawn. In many instances, the money you originally contribute to those plans is not currently subject to federal income tax.

If you have high amounts of earned income, you should consider establishing an IRA. Anyone with income from self-employment should consider contributing to a self-employed retirement account, such as a Keogh or SEP plan. And anyone whose employers offer a 401(k) plan or a thrift plan should be sure to participate to the maximum extent.

ANNUITIES

As you approach retirement, you might also want to consider a device offered by many insurance companies called an annuity. Annuities have become another option for investors wanting to build their retirement nest egg.

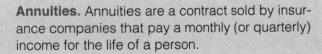

Annuities. Annuities are a contract sold by insurance companies that pay a monthly (or quarterly) income for the life of a person.

Annuities are life insurance with a twist; they are not actually life insurance, they are a contract with a life insurance company to pay benefits. While life insurance protects your dependents in the event of your death, an annuity covers the risk that you will live longer than expected. An annuity pays you a fixed amount of money each year for the rest of your life, or some other period that you have selected, regardless of how long you live.

An annuity is a tax-deferred investment contract that is underwritten by an insurance company. Although annuities come in a variety of types, the two primary types are immediate annuities and deferred annuities.

- **Immediate Annuity.** You usually purchase this contract with a lump-sum amount and begin receiving benefits 30 to 90 days later.

- **Deferred Annuity.** This contract pays you benefits starting at a future date, usually retirement.

You buy your annuity contract either by paying lump-sum payments, by making installment payments, or by a combination of the two. With a fixed annuity, the amount you receive is paid in regular, equal installments. You decide how frequently you want to receive payments (monthly, quarterly, or annually). That payment can be over a fixed period, such as 20 years, or for the rest of your life.

VARIABLE ANNUITIES

The most popular annuity for retirement investors is a variable deferred annuity. Variable annuities allow you to invest in a portfolio of investment options (such as guaranteed interest contracts or bond and stock mutual funds) that you select.

With a variable annuity, the interest, dividends, and capital gains you earn accumulate tax-deferred until they're paid to you under the terms of your annuity.

tip As with a Keogh, IRA, or other device that allows you to defer taxes, the price for tax deferral with an annuity is the same 10 percent penalty. You will pay ordinary income taxes plus a 10 percent penalty if you take the money out of an annuity before you reach the age 59 and a half.

ANNUITIES CAN BE EXPENSIVE

Annuities have their advantages if you want tax-deferred growth, but can be an expensive way to buy your investments. Above any sales commissions you pay to get in, these contracts (like mutual funds) charge investment management fees and have administrative costs. Because they also offer a death benefit, these contracts charge for the life insurance protection.

! There may also be surrender charges imposed if you take funds out of the contract too soon. All of these fees are in addition to those charged by the funds themselves. It may be a long time before the benefits of the tax deferral outweigh the commissions and additional costs.

In this lesson, you learned the importance of tax-deferred, tax-exempt, and tax-free income as you approach your retirement. In the next lesson, you will learn about real estate investments that may help you build your retirement nest egg in the years remaining prior to retirement.

ASSET
ALLOCATION

In this lesson, you will learn that it is important to allocate your assets among a select variety of investments to take the most advantage of the short time you have before you retire.

ALLOCATING ASSETS FOR SAFETY

Ironically, many people spend very little time on the asset allocation decision. Instead, they devote most of their energies toward trying to discover meaningful differences among particular investments or mutual funds.

Savvy investors, on the other hand, initially put aside considerations of which individual mutual fund, which stock, or which hard assets to own and focus on their portfolio allocation.

Asset Allocation. Asset allocation is the process of dividing your investable assets among the various investment categories in the most appropriate manner given your retirement goals, your need for current income, and the time horizon you have until you will need the money.

PROPER ALLOCATION

How do you, as someone over the age of 40, determine the allocation of assets that is right for your unique situation? There are four basic factors to consider:

- **Your tolerance for risk.** This is called the "sleep-at-night" factor. Risk tolerance is often hard to measure because it involves complex psychological factors. Essentially, only you know how you feel about risk, but most people are very risk-adverse and don't want to lose money.

- **Your age and investment horizon.** This is probably the most critical factor. Your time horizon to a particular goal governs the amount of risk you should take with your investments. It is also a major factor in the rate of return you will need to achieve your goals.

- **The phase of your investment cycle (accumulation or distribution).** If you're in the accumulation phase, you can have more growth-oriented investments in your portfolio and still manage market risk. However, you don't want to be selling your growth-oriented investments in volatile markets because of a need to generate current income.

- **Other factors, such as large concentrations in company stock.** Sometimes corporate employees have large amounts of company stock that they don't want to sell due to company potential or other factors. Asset allocation should take into account the need for additional diversification within the equity category given the large amount of business risk these individuals will be taking.

PERSONAL RISK TOLERANCE

Your asset allocation decisions will be influenced by your atti-
tude toward investment risk. Because perceptions of risk vary
from one investor to the next, two individuals with essentially
identical profiles (same income levels, same financial goals,
same Social Security benefits, and the same level of savings)
may choose to adopt quite different asset allocations.

Unfortunately, getting a feel for your own level of risk tolerance is not easy. There is no risk scale to indicate whether
you're a conservative, moderate, or aggressive investor.

YOUR PERSONAL FINANCIAL RESOURCES

Your personal financial situation will be the final factor that
influences your asset allocation decisions. If you feel that your
financial situation is tenuous (for example, if your company
has been experiencing layoffs), you may want to reduce your
investment risk. On the other hand, if your finances are on a
sound footing, you may be able to assume a higher level of
investment risk.

tip   When evaluating your financial situation, you
should consider factors such as the stability of
your job and career, your current income relative
to your income needs, your level of emergency
savings, and any additional income sources that
will be available to you during your retirement.

One method of allocating assets is the use of special funds that
exist for that very purpose.

Asset Allocation Funds

Some mutual funds invest in stocks, bonds, money markets, and real estate markets, so that any one market's losses may be offset by another's gain. In general, asset allocation mutual funds are supposed to represent a one-stop fund for investors who want all of the advantages of diversification in one account.

The Role of ESOPs in Asset Allocation

Ownership of stock in your employer's company potentially can leave your asset allocation seriously out of balance. Suppose, for example, that stock in your company represents 50 percent of the value of your total investments. You have decided that the appropriate asset allocation for your portfolio is 50 percent stocks, 40 percent bonds, and 10 percent hard assets. Does that mean you shouldn't own any other stocks? Usually, it's best to ignore the value of employer stock for asset allocation purposes. Otherwise, you may find yourself dangerously underdiversified.

In this example, you would apportion the half of your portfolio that is not employer stock according to that 50-40-10 allocation of stocks, bonds, and hard assets to allow for sufficient diversity in your stock investments.

Investment Objectives

If you're planning to retire in less than 20 years, your primary objective is to accumulate sufficient assets during your working years to maintain your standard of living during your retirement years. The gradual shift from accumulating assets to spending assets is known as the investment life cycle.

In investment terms, your objective during the accumulation years is to achieve growth of your capital; your emphasis during the distributive years of retirement shifts to income generation plus a modest level of capital growth to protect against inflation.

Along with your primary retirement objectives, you should have a secondary objective as well; short-term liquidity. Most financial planners recommend that, in addition to your longer-term retirement savings, you should maintain an emergency fund in a nonretirement account equal to three to six months of living expenses during your working years and six months to one year worth of living expenses during your retirement years. Naturally, this reserve should be separate and distinct from any short-term reserves held in your retirement portfolio.

INVESTMENT HORIZON

Your investment horizon can be measured in the scale of a human life span. On average, most individuals who reach the traditional retirement age of 65 will live into their 80s. Thus, when you begin to save for retirement in your 40s and 50s, you still have an investment horizon of three to four decades.

YOUR LIFE SPAN

As you age, your investment horizon obviously diminishes; by the time your reach your 80s, it may extend 10 years or less. If you plan to leave a portion of your retirement savings to your heirs, however, your investment horizon will extend well beyond your own life span.

In contemplating your likely investment horizon, an important factor to consider is your own family history. If members of your family have lived into their 90s and you (and your spouse) are in good health, you probably should plan on your investment horizon extending through age 100.

Although a 100 percent stock portfolio may be appropriate for accumulation investors in the earliest stages of the investment life cycle, few investors want to commit all of their savings to stocks. However, with a relatively short period of time to go before retirement, your objectives are twofold: you'll want (or need) to accumulate assets for retirement; and you'll want to preserve the capital you have accumulated so far.

While stocks may be your primary investment vehicle, it may also be time to realize some stock market gains and gradually move to a more conservative investment stance. Your recommended, extremely conservative, asset allocation might approximate 60 percent common stocks, 40 percent in bonds.

EARLY RETIREMENT YEARS

During retirement, you will begin to spend the capital you have accumulated. At the same time, your investment horizon may still extend (given current life expectations) 20 or 30 years. You'll need some growth in savings to protect your assets against inflation.

In this situation, it seems appropriate to reduce your common stock commitment while moving some of your assets into shorter-term reserves. Your recommended asset allocation would be 40 percent stocks, 40 percent bonds, and 20 percent cash or short-term reserves.

In this lesson, you learned the importance of allocating your retirement assets to produce the mix of growth, income, and risk that you're comfortable with as you strive to reach your retirement goals. In the next lesson, you will learn about the many strategies that can substantially increase your retirement assets and make the allocation of those assets more profitable.

INVESTMENT STRATEGIES

In this lesson, you will learn how to use investment strategies to maximize your return of conservative, value-retentive assets.

INVESTMENT FUNDAMENTALS

Many investors don't fully understand the fundamentals of investing and therefore may have unrealistic expectations about an investment's future performance. For example, money market mutual funds represent a low-risk haven for emergency reserves and should not be expected to match the performance of more volatile bonds.

Likewise, bonds or bond funds may not generate the growth you need if you're retiring in 20 years or less. While the steady decline in interest rates that began in the mid-1980s has resulted in substantial capital returns for bonds funds, inexperienced investors may view these yield-driven price gains as a sustainable component of the investment returns on bond funds. When interest rates reverse their protracted decline, these investors may be severely disappointed.

> When it comes to stocks and stock mutual funds, don't be fooled into believing that the 15 percent annual returns earned on stock investments during the past decade are normal.

In fact, these returns are well above the +10 percent historical average. When you understand how to analyze an investment's past performance records and its expected role in your retirement plan, you must learn about investment strategies and how they apply to those investments you have selected.

FINANCIAL RATIOS

Instead of getting hung up on the price of a stock or another investment, look at financial ratios that tell you the company's earnings per share or the value of assets per share.

Use the price in its proper perspective to compare it to other factors in similar companies of comparable size.

> **Ratio Analysis.** Ratio analysis is used in making credit judgments utilizing the relationship of figures to determine values and evaluate risks. In other words, converting figures into ratios permits apples and oranges to be compared or, in this case, to compare the value of two different sized companies.

STOCK INVESTING STRATEGIES

When it comes to investing in stocks, there are a number of basic facts that you should be aware of, all of which will help improve your results when investing. Consider, for example, the following truisms:

- You can't forecast day-to-day price changes. Most stocks merely move in the direction of the overall market. Developments in a particular industry may also affect the prices of stocks in that sector, as may a number of unanticipated factors.

- Over the long term, which can be 5 or 10 years or longer in your case, there's an uncanny correlation between share price and a company's profitability. Given this link, it is important to focus on a company's profits (also called earnings) before investing in any stock. The absolute size of a company's profits won't tell you much. What is important are profits in relation to the number of shares outstanding—in other words, earnings per share (EPS).

- Dividing earnings by the average number of common stock shares outstanding during the period being measured gives you the EPS figure. Look for companies with a pattern of EPS growth over at least five years and a habit of reinvesting 35 percent or more of earnings in expansion of the business.

tip You can determine the reinvestment rate by comparing EPS with the dividend payment. Earnings that aren't paid out to shareholders get reinvested in the business.

- Stocks are not all equally valued. You can get an idea of which are cheap and which are expensive by checking how each stock is priced in relation to its earnings. A measure of stock's price compared with others is its price/earnings ratio (P/E). The P/E is an indication of whether a stock is cheap or expensive and is probably the single most important number you can know about a stock.

Price/Earning Ratio. The P/E is the price of a share divided by the company's earnings per share. If a stock sells for $35 per share and the company earned $3.50 per share for the previous 12 months, the stock has a P/E ratio of 10. The P/E indicates how much investors are willing to pay for each dollar per share that the company earns.

The easiest way to find a company's P/E ratio is in the newspaper stock tables next to the stock's price. Unfortunately, what you see may not be too useful. For one thing, the numbers may reflect one time factors, such as earnings write-offs or asset sales, that temporarily deflate or inflate a company's profitability.

- There is no hard-and-fast rule for interpreting P/E ratios. You can, however, use one or more of the following analytical techniques:

    Think small. A low P/E may indicate an undervalued stock. Over long periods, stocks with low P/Es deliver surprising returns. But there is no rule that says that a cheap stock won't simply get cheaper.

Look at similar stocks. If most drug companies have P/Es of 20 but one trades for a P/E of 16, then that one might be undervalued (all other things being equal). Naturally, you don't want to make such comparisons of companies in dissimilar industries.

Compare growth with P/E. You'll rarely see a company with steadily increasing earnings and a below-average P/E ratio because investors pay up for the likelihood that the company will deliver high profits. Those profits will later lower the P/E based on today's price.

BOND STRATEGIES

You will discover that bonds can't match the performance record of stocks even over the period remaining before your retirement.

But they have performed well over shorter time periods—particularly since the 1980s. Because bonds should play a role in your retirement plans, you should consider a number of bond purchase techniques.

- Don't buy bonds when interest rates are low or rising. Stick with stocks or put your cash in CDs that mature in three to nine months. The ideal time to buy bonds is when interest rates have stabilized at a relatively high level or when they seem about to head down.

- Diversify by acquiring bonds with different maturity dates or bond funds with different average maturities. Short- and intermediate-term issues fluctuate less in price than longer-term issues, and they don't require you to tie up your money for 10 or more years in exchange for a relatively small additional yield.

- Don't buy any bond with a safety rating less than A and watch for news that may affect the rating while you own the bond. The worst thing that can happen to a bond that you own is that its issuer goes broke.

tip To check the rating of any bond you're considering, ask your broker or look it up in any one of several bond guides (such as Standard & Poor's or Moody's Investors' Guide) found in many libraries.

- For maximum safety, stick with bonds issued by the U.S. Treasury. To buy them commission free, set up an account through a program called Treasury Direct. For details, contact you nearest Federal Reserve bank branch or call the Bureau of Public Debt in Washington, DC, at 202-874-4000.

- Watch for the bond's call provisions. Some bonds can be called, which means that they can be redeemed by the issuer before they mature.

! A company might decide to call its bonds, for example, if interest rates fall so far that it could issue new bonds at a lower price (and thus save money). Call prices are good for the issuer but bad for investors. Not only would you lose comparatively high yield, you would also have to figure out where to invest the unexpected payment. Treasury issues are generally not callable.

> **tip** Because they provide automatic diversification, well-chosen mutual funds are often a better choice than individual stocks or bonds for investors who have small amounts to invest or who are just starting a retirement portfolio.

MUTUAL FUND STRATEGIES

Mutual funds let small investors hire professional money managers to take over the grunt work of investing, such as wading through reports on thousands of individual companies to compile a suitable investment portfolio.

With more than 4,500 mutual funds available today, how do you choose the one best suited to your needs? Begin by comparing the fund's 5- and 10-year returns. You want to see how the fund you're considering has performed in both bull and bear markets.

Bull. This is a person who thinks prices will rise. In a general sense, bullish means "optimistic."

Bear. This is a person who thinks that the market will fall. In other words, more pessimistic than a bull.

The foundation of your retirement portfolio should consist of a diversified equity fund invested in U.S. common stocks and a diversified bond fund invested in investment-grade U.S. bonds.

Return and risk matter most when it comes to selecting a mutual fund. You may not want to be aware of other factors, such as the fund's turnover rate (the average length of time that the fund holds shares before selling them).

> ! A high turnover rate sometimes indicates that the fund manager is trying to time the market (that is, judge when the market is going up or down), and market timing just doesn't work consistently.

In this lesson, you learned some of the basic investment strategies that you need to be aware of to maximize your investment return between now and your retirement date. In the next lesson, you will learn about more strategies that can help you increase the yield of your investments.

More Investment Strategies

In this lesson, you will learn more about the investment strategies that can help you maximize the earnings and profits from your retirement portfolio—without increasing the risk or the asset allocation of those investments.

Risk versus Return

Even given the brief period of time between now and your retirement, you can accept a lesser investment return while still reaching your financial goal. With only a few years to go, however, you may find yourself pressed to seek a higher return in order to attain your goal.

Risk. Risk is generally equated with a price fluctuation or, more accurately, the volatility of total return. Slight changes in return up or down each year denote lower risk, while wider swings constitute higher risk.

Return. Return is the gain you make on an investment and your earnings; it's how much you are ahead. With a bank savings account, your return is the amount of interest you collect.

The principal of your investment is guaranteed not to vary, so there is no gain or loss in value to add into the return equation. Buy a riskier type of investment, such as a corporate bond, however, and the price may rise or fall before you sell it. This increased risk is usually compensated by a higher return.

In that case, your return would have two elements: the amount of interest you receive plus or minus any gain or loss on the bond's price if it is sold before maturity.

MARKET RISK

Market Risk. Market risk is the danger that financial markets can rise or fall in value. As they do, these markets affect the value of a particular investment in the market even though the other risk factors for that investment may remain unchanged.

You may buy the stock of a prosperous company, for example, but the entire market may fall as a result of uncertainties about the economy. While your company may be doing quite well, investors will become wary of stocks in general, so the price of your stock will fall due to less demand.

You can protect yourself from volatility by investing for the long term, 5 or 10 years if you don't have much time before retirement. Over longer periods, the stock market's ups and downs have been more moderate than today's dramatic short-term ups and downs would seem to indicate.

MARKET TIMING

As the period during which you must accumulate retirement assets shortens, you may want to eliminate market risk by "timing the market."

 Market Timing. This is predicting where the market is going and reacting accordingly. Generally, people who try to determine market changes (called market timers) do not consistently make the right call. In essence, market timing is sophisticated guessing.

PURCHASING POWER RISK

One of the biggest risks to your long-term retirement security is purchasing power risk.

 Purchasing Power Risk. The risk that your money won't keep pace with inflation.

To reduce purchasing power risk now or after retirement, you should invest for the long term in assets whose returns have traditionally outpaced inflation, such as common stocks. You should invest to maintain a real rate of return over your investment time horizon, retirement, and beyond.

> *tip* How do you calculate your real return? Figure your after-tax rate of return and then subtract the current rate of inflation. The result is your real rate of return.

By focusing on your real rate of return, you can calculate whether your investments are staying ahead of inflation. Investment experts point out that a one to four percent real rate of return in a moderately risky portfolio mix is a significant accomplishment.

MARKET TIMING TECHNIQUES

There are two basic market timing techniques used by some investors: dollar cost averaging and fixed amount investing. If you are investing in individual stocks, these timing techniques may not be practical for you. These techniques, however, can be quite useful for timing mutual fund investments.

 Dollar Cost Averaging. This is a strategy of investing the same dollar amount in the same investment at fixed time intervals.

> *tip* Investors usually have the option of investing in mutual funds in relatively small dollar amounts. Sometimes, they will make an agreement with a fund to send in a fixed dollar amount every month to that fund. This adds discipline to their savings strategy. It also helps them establish a better cost basis for the fund.

When you send in a set dollar amount every month, you will buy fewer shares when the price of shares goes up and more shares when the price goes down. You end up dollar cost averaging your price per share.

If the investment goes through a down cycle, you will be buying more shares while it is down, thus reducing the average cost per share over that time. If it goes up, you will be buying fewer shares at the higher price.

> *tip* You should note that if the price of the investment only goes up after the initial investment, you would end up cost averaging a higher price per share— but it would still be profitable.

 Fixed Amount Investing. This is simply the strategy of keeping a constant dollar amount invested at certain time intervals, such as six months or a year.

Using the fixed amount investing strategy, you would sell shares if the total amount of the investment went over the original amount you put in, and you would buy more shares if it went down.

A variation of fixed amount investing is fixed ratio investing. This is a strategy often used by institutional investors for keeping the same ratio of stocks to bonds in a portfolio at all times. Typically, someone who uses a fixed ratio investing strategy will keep 50 percent of their investment capital in stocks and 50 percent in bonds. If the stock portion of their portfolio rises, they will sell stock and buy bonds to keep the ratio at

50-50. If the stock portion drops, the investor would sell bonds and buy stocks to keep the 50-50 mix.

ECONOMIC CYCLES

Fundamental analysis deals primarily with forecasting economic trends and cycles.

 Economic Cycle. An economic cycle is a period of either sustained inflation or recession. Inflation means that the price of most goods and services is rising and the size of the total economic base is expanding.

INVESTMENT EVALUATION STRATEGIES

There are two theories about the analysis of investments:

- **Fundamental Analysis.** The basic premise of fundamental analysis is that the most important consideration for selecting a good stock for investment is the future earnings potential of the company.

- **Technical Analysis.** This is the method of selecting good investments primarily on the basis of supply and demand factors. Technical analysis also relies heavily on interpreting chart patterns of the past performance of the stock's price.

To forecast a particular company's earnings, you must also take into account the outlook for the economy as a whole and the outlook for the industry in which that company is involved.

Reading and analyzing financial statements and studying economic cycles and industry trends are disciplines of fundamental analysis. By far the single most important factor in fundamental analysis is the direction of interest rates.

> **tip** If you want to be a good student of the stock market, you must first be a good student of interest rates. As with bonds, there is a direct cause-and-effect inverse relationship between interest rates and stock prices. As interest rates rise, stock prices drop. This is due, in part, to the fact that a rise in interest rates will generally result in a decrease in many companies' earnings.

TECHNICAL ANALYSIS

As mentioned, technical analysis involves methods of studying indicators that are intended to predict whether the supply of shares that will be offered for sale will be satisfied by the expected demand for those shares.

Someone who relies heavily on technical analysis for evaluating their investments is often referred to as a "pure technician."

Most investors use fundamental analysis to select what to invest in and use technical analysis to help them decide when to invest in it. Technical analysis is most valuable for offering guidelines in investment timing.

In this lesson, you learned that there are many strategies for investing in stocks, bonds, and mutual funds. In the next lesson, you will learn how to keep track of your retirement assets between now and retirement.

MONITORING THROUGH RETIREMENT

In this lesson, you will learn that retirement planning is an ongoing process that requires monitoring and fine-tuning up to and beyond retirement.

CONSTANT MONITORING

Monitoring your retirement portfolio does not mean switching assets every time the market declines or shuffling mutual funds on a regular basis. That kind of hands-on strategy will usually produce only high commissions and fees. Instead, with your retirement plan in place, you have to make certain that it stays on track until and after retirement.

YOUR RETIREMENT PLAN'S VITAL SIGNS

There are quite a few things that will impact your retirement plan. You must, for example, consider the impact of inflation. There is also the matter of taxes to consider. Above all, it is necessary to periodically reassess your retirement portfolio.

You have to watch out for inflation. Inflation can inflict irreparable damage by steadily chewing up a chunk of your nest egg's value. Even the seemingly low levels of inflation of recent years can cause significant damage between now and retirement.

> *tip*   Owning stocks and stock mutual funds will be your best long-term defense against inflation. These investments have managed to gain a yearly average of more than 10 percent since 1926, which is a comfortable margin above the rate of inflation.

While you may have to pay tax on some or all of your stock earnings each year if the investments aren't held in a tax-sheltered account, stocks and stock funds will generate the bulk of their return in appreciation and there's no tax due on that until you sell the stock.

> *tip*   When taxes are due, you should consider paying the bill from separate funds rather than using the money in your retirement nest egg. That keeps your retirement money compounding at top speed and puts you well ahead of inflation.

REASSESS WHENEVER NECESSARY

A job change, a big promotion, an inheritance, a divorce or marriage, a child who wants to attend an expensive private college, or one who doesn't, are all events that can change the shape of your retirement finances fast. To keep your plan on track, recalculate your retirement income goal and the assets you already have whenever a major change happens.

> **tip** It's a good idea to recalculate every few years even if there haven't been any big changes.

Divorce

No matter what your age, the pension you accumulate at work will probably be considered an asset to be divided with your spouse if you are later divorced.

If you untie the knot at age 50, for example, a portion of the benefits you stand to collect at retirement could belong to your ex-spouse under what is known among divorce lawyers as a qualified domestic relations order, or QDRO (pronounced kwa-dro).

> **tip** On the flip side, you may be able to collect a portion of your ex's pension from his or her employer.

Death of a Spouse

After the death of a spouse, you will need to amend your insurance coverage. If your spouse handled your insurance, you may be unfamiliar with the process. In any event, it will pay to talk with a competent insurance adviser.

In addition to reviewing and changing the beneficiary designations on existing policies, you have to assess your own insurance needs as a result of the changed circumstances.

- If you were formerly covered as a spouse under a health insurance plan, continuing coverage will have to be arranged. Appropriate coverage will have to be acquired.

- Appropriate coverage in your name for auto, homeowner's or renter's, and umbrella liability insurance is also necessary.

- Depending on individual circumstances, you may need to adjust or increase the limits on disability and life insurance coverage.

ANTICIPATING THE WORST

With relatively little time to go until retirement, it becomes imperative that you not only have a viable plan for your estate but that you also monitor it in light of your changing circumstances.

Keeping abreast of the outside factors that might affect your estate plan (such as law and rule changes), requires understanding the phrases that you'll learn more about in the next lesson. For the time being, you should understand these terms because they are used so frequently in estate planning:

- **Decedent.** A recently deceased person.

- **Estate.** The property belonging to the decedent, such as investments, real estate, and personal property, at the time of his or her death.

CHECK SOCIAL SECURITY

You should occasionally check your Social Security records for mistakes and request a change if you find any. After all, retirement is fast approaching and you don't want any surprises that might delay receipt of that Social Security check.

> *tip* Call 800-772-1213 and request Form 7004-SM, the Request for Earnings and Benefits Estimate Statement. About four weeks after you mail back the form, you should receive an estimate of your retirement benefits along with a year-by-year listing of your Social Security earnings.

PERFORMANCE TRACKING

It is vitally important to continue monitoring your retirement portfolio. You shouldn't be a fanatic about it; there's no need to check the stock and mutual fund tables every day. After all, this is a 5-, 10-, or 15-year proposition and paying too close attention can be just as damaging as ignoring it completely.

> *tip* You can't ignore investment performance. Remember, everybody makes a bad choice now and again.

Your approach can be as simple as reading the quarterly and annual reports you'll receive from the stocks and funds you own as well as a few investment publications. Or, you can plug all of the information into a general money-management software computer program that will make all of the key calculations for you.

SAVINGS AND DEBT

Rushing to realize your retirement planning goals means amassing all of the funds, investments, and assets you can in the years just ahead. Damaging debt, in the form of increasing credit card balances, can sap those funds that could otherwise go to retirement savings.

Watch those plastic balances to avoid paying unnecessary interest and channel the savings into your nest egg. You might even consider a plan to pay off your home mortgage early and save thousands of dollars in interest costs.

MONITOR YOUR COMPANY

Your own retirement plan's pulse may be closely linked to your company's health. That is especially true if you participate in a profit-sharing plan at work, hold any of your retirement assets in company stock, or participate in an employee stock ownership plan (ESOP).

Read the company's annual and quarterly reports as well as outside media or analyst reports on the firm. If the company's growth prospects dim and other investment options are available for that money, consider switching your assets elsewhere.

In this lesson, you learned the importance of monitoring your retirement portfolio and making changes in it, depending on life events. In the next lesson, you will learn how you can direct the disposition of your assets while you are living and what you can plan for after death.

WHEN RETIREMENT IS IN SIGHT

In this lesson, you will learn that you shouldn't relax your planning efforts as you approach your planned retirement age.

EVALUATING AN EARLY RETIREMENT OFFER

The terms of every early retirement offer vary depending on whether it is a true voluntary early retirement program or an involuntary severance program.

Many voluntary early retirement offers provide employees with a host of benefits, from cash severance payments and enhanced pensions to post-retirement medical coverage and offers of counseling or help in finding a new job.

> **!** Check the specifics of your retirement offer. Remember, your company has no legal obligation to offer these payments and its program may be very different.

EARLY RETIREMENT CONSEQUENCES

If you're surprised by an early retirement offer, don't feel singled out or that it reflects your job performance. Particularly over the past 10 years, companies have increasingly used early retirement programs to reduce workforce levels across the board.

tip Keep in mind that you do have a choice. Under federal law, you can't be forced to take the package offered. However, nothing prevents your company from later eliminating your job, demoting you, or otherwise making you wish you had taken the offer.

Many companies follow up voluntary programs with a less generous involuntary severance program within a year or two. Also, if you want to work after you leave your current position (or expect you would have to) and you receive an early retirement offer, think about your odds of landing another job.

CAN YOU AFFORD TO RETIRE YET?

If you have good prospects for finding another job or starting your own business, the decision may be easy. But for many of you, the real question comes down to whether you can afford to retire now.

If you receive an early retirement offer, consider the following:

- Look at the pension benefits you will receive. Will you get lower benefits because you're retiring early or do enhanced age and years of service make up the difference?

- Will you receive enough to fund your retirement adequately until you qualify for Social Security benefits?

- How do your early retirement benefits compare with those you would collect if you continued to work for your company? Are they more generous or less generous?

- Medical benefits will become increasingly important to someone in their 60s.

In analyzing the offer, don't avoid the tougher questions:

- Does the bank still hold a mortgage on your house? If it does, can you still make the mortgage payments without working full-time?

- What about health care expenses? You'll need to pay for medical coverage if it isn't part of your early retirement offer.

- Do you anticipate income from other sources (an inheritance, perhaps) to increase your income in retirement years?

PENSION DISTRIBUTION OPTIONS

When retirement is in sight, you will be asked to make a number of decisions regarding how you want to receive your pension. Your goal with any such retirement distribution strategy is to maximize your income. Because a large portion of that income will probably come from your company retirement plan, maximizing your income really means understanding and making the appropriate decisions when it comes to your retirement plan withdrawals.

ANNUITY DISTRIBUTION OPTIONS

If your company has a defined benefit pension plan, it will provide several annuity or monthly payment distribution options. Some benefit plans will give you another choice when it comes to withdrawing your pension money: you may receive these in the form of an annuity or you may take a lump-sum distribution.

> **tip** Most pension plans offer employees a choice of several annuity payments. The basic pension benefit is a single life annuity.

> **Single Life Annuity.** The single life annuity is a payment spread over the life of the employee— you'll receive a monthly check for as long as you live. However, after you die, no further payments go to your survivors or your estate.
>
> This benefit is not usually indexed for inflation, which can reduce real income for someone who lives 20 to 30 years past their date of retirement.

Many married people prefer a joint and survivor (J&S) annuity, which pays benefits to you and your survivors as long as either of you live. Generally, your monthly payment will be reduced if you elect a J&S payment in exchange for a guaranteed payment to your survivors. The reduction depends on the age of the survivors. The younger the survivor, the larger the reduction.

WHAT TYPE OF ANNUITY IS BEST?

In selecting an annuity option, you should consider your marital status, the health and age of you and your spouse at the time you retire, the financial resources available to your surviving spouse, and whether you have any other beneficiaries you want to provide for.

> **!** Remember, federal law requires that both you and your spouse decide. If you are married and opt for anything other than a 50 percent or higher J&S with your spouse, then your spouse has to consent. This consent must be in the form of a notarized waiver that both you and your spouse have signed.

> **tip** If you and your spouse die when actuaries say you're supposed to, the total dollar amount is the same for both choices. In other words, single-life and joint and survivor annuities are designed to be actuarial equivalents.

ANNUITY VERSUS LUMP SUM

If your pension plan provides both annuity and lump-sum payment options, you have a difficult choice to make. Annuities and lump-sum distributions are designed to be "actuarially equivalent"—either way, you're supposed to get the same amount of money in the end.

However, annuities and lump sums are not equivalent if you die before or after the actuaries say you should. If you die sooner than your actuarial life expectancy, you're better off with a lump sum. If you die later, you're better off with an annuity.

> **tip**   If you take the lump sum and don't spend it down, you can pass it on to your children or other beneficiaries.

Another consideration is the rate of return you will get on your money. When you take an annuity, your company retirement plan takes responsibility for investing the money and the annuity payments are calculated assuming a particular investment rate of return. For most plans, those assumed rates range somewhere between five and eight percent. If you think you can beat this assumed rate of return, opt for a lump-sum payment.

LUMP-SUM DISTRIBUTIONS

While many company-sponsored benefit plans offer a choice between annuity or lump-sum distributions, all 401(k) plans provide only for lump sum distributions. Thus, you are likely to have at least one lump-sum distribution to deal with at the time you retire.

With lump-sum distributions, your main advantage is flexibility. A lump sum gives you many choices related to how you invest your money and pay your taxes. You also have an opportunity to leave your heirs a lump sum of money that isn't available with a pension annuity.

Maximizing your retirement income means making the best choice among the investment options that pertain to your personal situation.

LUMP-SUM TAXES

When it comes to income taxes, you can pay them up front when you receive the distribution and you may get a significant tax break if you qualify for forward averaging (that is if you qualify for five- or ten-year averaging). Or, you can roll over your funds into a rollover IRA and postpone paying your taxes until you take the money out of the IRA, losing the option of forward averaging.

> *tip* You can also combine your choices: roll over part of the lump-sum distribution to an IRA, thus deferring taxes on that portion, and pay taxes on the portion you don't roll over.

If you aren't retiring, only changing jobs, you may be able to simply transfer the lump sum to your new employer's plan. However, you have to be aware of the time limits imposed by tax rules. If the transfer or rollover into another qualified plan isn't accomplished within the time constraints or if the lump-sum payor isn't aware that the funds will be rolled over, the funds may be reduced by the 20 percent tax withholding.

> **!** If you take the money yourself and do not use a direct rollover, do not miss the 60-day deadline. If you do, the right to roll your distribution into an IRA is gone forever. The clock begins ticking the day you receive the check, so make copies of the check and postmarked envelopes for proof.

AVERAGING

In order to use either 5- or 10-year averaging, you must have a qualifying lump-sum distribution. If you don't meet the tests contained in the tax rules, you can't use averaging although you may still be able to roll your distribution into an IRA.

> **!** Under the rules, the distribution must be from a qualified retirement plan, such as a pension, 401(k), or profit-sharing plan in which you participate for at least five tax years. You cannot use averaging on a distribution from an IRA. Also, you must have separated from service with your employer or have attained age 59 and a half.

EXCESS DISTRIBUTION TAX

To further complicate your choices as retirement approaches, the IRS has another wrinkle for wealthy taxpayers in the form of a 15 percent additional tax on excess distributions.

To know if you're subject to the tax, add up all of your distributions from pensions and tax-deferred retirement accounts, such as your 401(k), Keogh, IRA, or ESOP. Exclude your Social Security benefits and any money that may represent after-tax contributions you made to the plan. Then, from this amount, subtract $150,000 (in 1996).

The amount that tops $150,000 is your excess distributions unless you've withdrawn a lump sum this year. In that case, your excess distribution is that amount.

In this lesson, you learned that planning does not end as retirement approaches. You also learned how to evaluate an early retirement offer to see whether you can afford to retire earlier than you planned.

INDEX